jewelry making
techniques book

Over 50 techniques for creating eyecatching
contemporary and traditional designs

ELIZABETH OLVER

NORTH LIGHT BOOKS
Cincinnati, Ohio

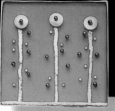

contents

A QUARTO BOOK

First published in North America in 2001
by North Light Books,
an imprint of F&W Publications, Inc.,
1507 Dana Avenue
Cincinnati, OH 45207

ISBN 1-58180-210-2

QUAR.JEMT

Conceived, designed, and produced by
Quarto Publishing plc
The Old Brewery
6 Blundell Street
London N7 9BH

Senior Project Editor Nicolette Linton
Art Editor/Designer Sheila Volpe
Assistant Art Director Penny Cobb
Photographer Paul Forrester
Text Editors Claire Waite, Vanessa Farquharson
Indexer Pamela Ellis

Art Director Moira Clinch
Publisher Piers Spence

Manufactured by Regent Publishing Services Ltd,
Hong Kong
Printed by Leefung-Asco Printers Ltd, China

Author's Acknowledgments
Miles, Beth, and Penge for their patience, help, and
support, without which this book could not have
been written.

For their expertise: Martin Baker, Graham Fuller,
John Harrison, Chris Howes, Fleur Klinkers,
Miriam Prescott, Vannetta Seecharran, Ron
Stevens, Roger Taylor, Paul Wells.

For the loan of tools, materials, and studio space:
Central Saint Martin's College of Art and Design,
EMC Services Ltd, Rashbel Ltd, Tony Jarvis Ltd,
and H.S. Walsh.

Repeated patinated steel forms undulate to entertain the eye in a necklace.

Introduction

My passion for making jewelry began in a metal workshop at school. I thoroughly enjoyed my time carving mother of pearl and soldering silver to make my first pair of earrings, little realizing at the time that I was sowing the seeds of my future.

One of the most important lessons that I learned from the skilled tutors and technicians at art school was that, beyond the ultimate need for patience, there is rarely a single definitive way of making jewelry. In fact, there are more likely to be 101 different interpretations and permutations on a theme.

The subcutaneous layer of oxidized wire creates a subtle surface pattern on this two-tone ring.

Ask three different people how they would perform the same task and you are likely to get three different answers. Don't be put off—choose the answer that most suits your way of thinking and doing, add the useful elements from the other two answers, give yourself a little time to hone your skills and gain experience, and you are likely to add a fourth solution to the equation!

A technique may have geographic and regional differences according to the expertise, tools, materials, and services that dominate the craft in that area. Even the most experienced jeweler can learn a new trick or have some small mystery explained when watching someone new tackle a familiar task.

Jewelry making is addictive because there is practically no end to the learning curve, although one need not—and indeed cannot—be a master in

Stones and other surface details are used to make patterns in these distinctive earrings.

The tactile surface of this uplifting ring conjures up delicious weather-worn treasures.

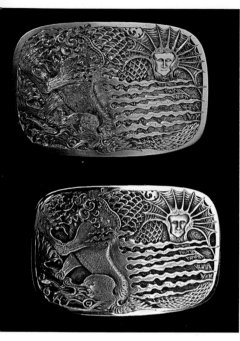

all areas since proficiency in some techniques can take many years of practice. As in all things in life, to be really good at anything you need to set your mind to the task and practice to perfect your skills.

However you choose to explore making jewelry, the important thing is to enjoy the process and the results. For some people this may be a Zen-like experience where perfection in every detail is a prerequisite; while for others it will involve the need for as near-instantaneous gratification as can be achieved with jewelry making. Whatever your approach, jewelry encompasses so many different skills and challenges there is likely to be something for everyone.

Feast your eyes on the detail in these intricate narrative brooches.

The modest bezel set stone contrasts with the fabulous proportions of this ring.

HOW TO USE THIS BOOK

Technique heading.

Example of a finished piece made using the technique.

Background information to the technique.

Equipment and materials you will need to complete the technique.

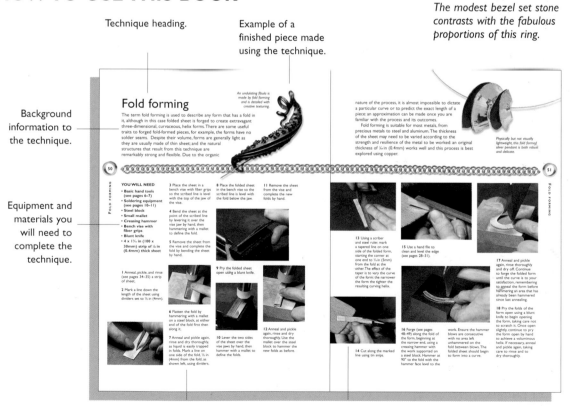

Copy explaining each stage of the technique.

Photograph showing the technique in action.

Basic hand tools

Many of the basic hand tools needed for jewelry-making have not changed in decades; some have not changed significantly in centuries. There are many tools beyond those shown here that will become useful as your skills increase and your horizons broaden; however, with a limited number of tools and skills, complex and beautiful jewelry can still be made.

To find all the tools in one place it is a good idea to visit a specialist jewelry-making tool store (see **Tools suppliers**, pages 124–125): buy metals from a bullion supplier and stones from a stone supplier (see **Bullion and stone suppliers**, pages 124–125). The cost of tools can vary a great deal according to the quality. It isn't necessary to buy top-quality tools from the outset, although it is advisable to buy the highest quality you can afford. You can build on your toolkit as your skills are expanded.

Bow drill

Twist drills

Archimedes drill

G–clamp

Bench peg and G–clamp
In the absence of a jeweler's bench (see page 10), you can start off by using a bench peg, a wooden attachment with a triangular cutout that allows for sawing, fixed to a sturdy table using a G–clamp. If you take up jewelry-making seriously then a jeweler's bench is infinitely preferable.

Bench peg

Fixed frame

Adjustable frame and saw blades

Saws: frames and blades
Jeweler's saw frames are either fixed or adjustable. The fixed frame is easier to tense as it is physically more flexible; the adjustable frame allows you to reuse shorter, broken saw blades. Jeweler's saw frames are much the same as those used for marquetry, dentistry, and in other trades where intricate cutting is necessary. Blades for jewelry saws are available in a variety of sizes; probably the most versatile blade is the 2/0, which is relatively fine yet robust. The finest 6/0 saw blades are used for very fine or detailed work. A general guide to choosing a blade is a minimum of 2½ teeth to the thickness of the metal.

Hand drill

Hand drills
Drills that can be used by hand, such as the bow drill or Archimedes drill, will be necessary if you do not have a mechanical drill such as a flexible shaft motor, also known as a pendant drill. The Archimedes, bow drill, and the traditional hand drill are limited in their usefulness as they require both hands of the maker to operate them and create the drilling action. Twist drills are the steel tool bits used in conjunction with hand drills to make holes.

Pin vise

**Tripoli
and rouge**

**Sanding sticks
and abrasive
papers**

**Polishing
stick**

Pin vise
A pin vise offers a means
of holding small tools that
are otherwise difficult
to use.

Files and file handles
Jewelry files are used for
removing excess material.
Various grades or cuts
are available for different
jobs and finishes. Large
jewelry files are generally
used for bigger jobs, while
the smaller needle files
are mostly used for more
intricate work. Although
round, square, triangular,
half-round, equaling, and
warding shape make a
good selection to start
out with, there are many
other shapes that you
may eventually need (see
pages 26–29). Files are
available in a number of
cuts from 0, the coarsest,
to 6, the finest. Cut 2 is
robust enough for most
jobs and is a useful cut
to start with. The best
quality files are costly and
can be damaged if stored
incorrectly: files should
not be placed in direct
contact with other files
or steel tools as these
can wear the cutting
surface. Mount the file
in a file handle for safety
and comfort.

Emery sticks, emery papers, and wet-and-dry sandpaper
Jewelers traditionally
used sanding papers
called emery paper.
Sanding sticks and papers
are used for cleaning up
after filing, soldering (see
pages 82–83).
   The longlasting and
tenacious silicone carbide
papers, also known as
wet-and-dry sandpaper,
have become increasingly
popular for the same
tasks. A number that
refers to the number of
grains to be found in a
given area indicates the
grade; 150 is coarse,
1200 is fine and used
as a polishing paper.
Though more costly than
emery papers they are
readily found, as they
are not exclusive to the
jewelry trade.

Polishing sticks, polishing compounds, and polishing threads
Felt or leather sticks are
used in combination with
polishing compounds
for hand polishing.
Store polishing tools
separately from files and
sanding tools to avoid
contamination, and label
your equipment to avoid
mixing them up.
   Tripoli and rouge are
polishing compounds:
essentially greasy
compounds containing
grit. Tripoli is the coarser
of the two compounds
and is used before rouge,
which gives the fine
mirror finish expected
of a high polish. It is
advisable to store
polishing compounds
separately.
   Polishing threads are
thin strands of cotton
that can be pulled
through small holes
to polish fretwork.

**Polishing
threads**

**Escapement
files**

**Needle
files**

Large files

File handles

Dividers

Scriber

Center punch

Tin snips

Top cutters

Engineering square

Steel ruler

Top cutters and tin snips
Top or end cutters are generally used for cutting wire, while tin snips are most often used for cutting sheet and solder. Avoid cutting materials that are harder than the cutting edge of your tin snips or cutters as this will damage the edge.

Safety glasses
Safety equipment is of paramount importance. You will find that good-quality safety goggles are essential as your eyes are particularly vulnerable during certain tasks, such as drilling, pickling, and etching with chemicals (see page 24).

Pliers
Pliers are used for holding and forming—shaping—pieces of jewelry. If you have flat-, round-, ring-, or flat-nosed parallel, and serrated-edge pliers in your toolbox you will be able to tackle most jobs and work with most materials. Pliers are worth investing in as they are hard wearing, lasting tools if used carefully. Store in dry conditions where they won't rust.

Engineering tools
Engineering tools, such as a steel ruler, a pair of dividers, an engineer's square, and a scriber are used for marking out and checking for accuracy in a number of different tasks. A center punch is used to make an initial hole when drilling.

Safety glasses

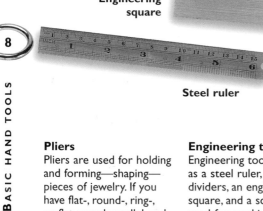

Pliers

Vernier caliper

Ring-nosed pliers

Parallel pliers

Caliper
Calipers are used for accurate measurement. They can be found in a variety of formats, from a sliding vernier caliper to a dial gauge caliper, or the more modern digital readout caliper.

Forming and soldering equipment

Jewelry-making is a wide subject so the direction of your interests will dictate how your toolkit expands. With each discipline you embrace you will need to add a few specific tools to your collection. If the opportunity arises, you can be introduced to specialized disciplines and tools through evening classes or summer schools, where the hands-on approach may well inform your choices.

Planishing hammer

Bangle mandrel

FORMING TOOLS

Forming metal, basically maneuvering it into a desired shape, is sometimes possible with just a pair of pliers. Simple formers, such as mallets, hammers, mandrels, and doming blocks, will allow you to form a wider variety of metal shapes.

Mandrels

Metal formers—called mandrels or triblets—are used for forming shapes such as rings and bangles. These come in different sizes and profiles.

Creasing hammer

Mallets

Wood or leather mallets allow you to apply force without stretching the metal. The wooden or leather head is softer than the metal so tends not to mark the surface.

Hammers

Metal hammers can stretch the metal you are working with as well as polish and texture the surface, according to the shape and finish of the hammer face. There are many varieties of jeweler's hammer, including the

Raising hammer

planishing hammer, used to impart a polish to metal, pin hammers, used in riveting, and blocking, raising, and creasing hammers for various forming and forging techniques (see pages 48–51).

Doming block and doming punches

Circles of metal can be placed into the hollows of a doming block and easily punched into domes using doming punches (see page 36). Wooden punches do not stretch the metal, although they tend not to last as long as metal punches.

Leather mallet

Doming block

Wood mallets

Doming punches

Ring mandrel

Steel block and riveting hammer

Pickle bath, tongs, and safety glasses.

Steel block
The perfect flat surface of a steel block is useful for flattening sheet and wire, or to support work as it is forged (see pages 48–49), riveted (see page 112), or textured (see page 91) with punches (see above) or hammers.

Swage block
Use a swage block with metal doming punches (see above) to make tubes or fashion curved gully forms (see page 37).

Swage block

French/Dutch torch

Propane canister torch

SOLDERING EQUIPMENT
Soldering equipment significantly broadens the spectrum of jewelry construction. Annealing (the softening of metal) and soldering (the joining of metal) share many of the same tools and equipment, although for soldering you will require all of this equipment and more as your skills grow. After soldering or annealing, pickle your work in a chemical solution to remove the oxides that form on the surface of the metal due to heating (see page 35).

Soldering torches
There are a number of soldering torches readily available. A compact handheld micro torch makes an effective portable torch for small-scale work, up to 1 troy oz (31g). It is easily filled with butane gas. For larger work, you may consider using a French/Dutch torch that requires an air supply, by puffs of breath or using bellows, to fuel the heat of a soft flame. A propane canister torch can be fitted with different size nozzles to cope with small or larger scale work.

Water jar

250 mL
±5%
PYREX®
U.S.A

Water jar
A jar of water is useful at the bench for quenching —cooling—a recently heated metal (see pages 34–35).

Pickle solution
Pickle solutions are used to remove oxides from metal (see page 35 for details).

Pickle bath and pickle tongs
A ceramic or Pyrex dish over a candle or nightlight works well as a pickling devise: low heat accelerates the pickling process. For large work a covered Pyrex dish over a low heat or an electric ceramic casserole that has thermostatic control can be used. Safety glasses are essential as splashback may occur if work is dropped into the pickle solution, and it is also a good idea to wear heavy duty rubber gloves. Pickle tongs can be found made of plastic, wood, copper, or brass. If tongs are made of steel, check they are specifically marked as pickle tongs—ordinary steel should not be used in pickle as it creates an adverse reaction.

Tweezers
Tweezers are useful for holding or handling work while annealing, soldering, and pickling. Brass tweezers can be used in pickle, while sprung-arm tweezers keep their hold once the handles have been released.

Sprung-arm tweezers

Brass tweezers

Flux dish, soldering brush, probe, mesh, block, mat, and micro torch

Steel mesh
A steel mesh allows heat to circulate around an object while soldering or annealing on top of a soldering mat or block.

Binding wire
This wire is used bind pieces of metal together for soldering.

Charcoal block, turntable, and binding wire

Flux and flux dish (borax and borax dish)
Flux is used in conjunction with solder to prevent oxidization, which blackens metal. The most commonly found and used flux is borax, which comes in the form of a cone that is ground with water in a special dish for the purpose.

Flux brush
Use a dedicated brush to apply flux to your work while soldering. Don't use it for any other purpose.

Solder probe
A solder probe is a useful tool for manipulating hot work or solder.

Soldering mat, soldering block, and charcoal block
Soldering mats are made from various non-flammable materials and are used to protect your bench and support your work and tools while soldering. A soldering block is a thicker version of the soldering mat and raises your work. Traditionally a charcoal block was used because it radiates heat, but is an expensive luxury now.

Turntable
A turntable is a useful piece of equipment because it allows you to rotate work during the soldering process.

Solder
Solder is found in different grades for different metals, and is bought from a bullion dealer or some jewelry tool suppliers.

Pins and tacks
These can be used as aids to tack work or hold awkward shapes in place while soldering.

Strips of solder

Borax cone dish

Sheets of solder

Pins

Tacks

Furnishing a basic studio

Jewelry-making doesn't require huge pieces of furniture or equipment, so it can be carried out in relatively small spaces. Beyond the items shown here, a chest with small drawers will allow you to keep tools and materials in order. Small containers are also useful for keeping findings or jump rings, for example. A good light source is necessary so that you don't strain your eyes, although direct sunlight can cause difficulty when soldering.

Draw plate

Ring stick and gauges

Bench vise

Jeweler's bench
An important piece of furniture that you may consider investing in is a jeweler's bench, along with a comfortable chair. The bench top looks higher than you might expect; ideally your elbows should lie just below shoulder height when you are sitting at the bench, otherwise you will find yourself stooping over your work. The jeweler's bench's hemispherical cutout allows you to work over a hide or drawer which is used to collect scrap and filings, as well as protecting you from hot or sharp objects that may fall from the bench top. Organize your tools and work space so that everything is within reach without cluttering up the workbench, which can result in accidents.

Bench brush
Any small brush of reasonable quality, such as a wide household paintbrush, can be used to clean the bench after work.

Fiber grips

Bench vise and fiber grips
A bench vise is used for holding items firmly while you work, for example holding a draw plate on the bench while you draw

Jeweler's bench

wire through it (see below). The fiber grips will protect your work from the steel jaws of the vise which can damage it, especially if they are serrated. A 2½ in (6.5cm) jaw vise with a clamp can be used at the bench; a larger 4 in (10cm) jaw vise has greater strength, although it will need a fixed mounting.

Ring stick and gauges
A ring stick with sizes marked up the taper help with sizing rings. Ring gauges—to be passed over the finger—can be found in wide or narrow format: wide rings need to be sized slightly larger to pass over the knuckle.

Draw plate
This is a steel tool used for decreasing the size or changing the shape of wire. The steel plate features a series of holes of decreasing size. On the reverse side of the draw plate the holes are opened as access for the tapered wire to be fed through the hole for drawing. Draw plates can be bought to form in almost any shape.

Sandbag
A leather sandbag has a soft backing but gives resistance. It is used as a means of supporting work while hammering, or for supporting a repoussé bowl (see pages 52–53).

Sandbag

Wax rasps

File handle

Wire wool

WAX CARVING TOOLS

Wax carving creates three-dimensional forms for casting (see pages 72–73). These days, a special plastic is used, but it is referred to as wax.

Rasps

Rasps are coarser than files and can grate wax to quickly remove it.

Saw blades for wax

Spiral saw blades are used specifically for wax carving because the wax does not clog behind the cut just made.

Wire wool

Wire wool is available in different grades. Fine wire wool is used to polish the surface of wax.

Dental tools

Dental tools are available in a range of different-shaped heads that allow you to scrape and carve intricate detail.

SETTING TOOLS

Setting requires a number of specialist tools to prepare work, to hold the work, and to apply pressure during the stone setting process.

Acetone

Acetone is a chemical used to remove residual setter's wax once the work is released.

Ring clamp

Ring clamps are used to support and hold a ring firmly during the setting process. A ring clamp will only support more traditional ring forms. Other forms will need to be set up with setter's wax on a file handle or another suitable base, commonly made from wood.

Setter's wax

Combination stone

Setter's wax

Setter's wax is a cement used to hold work while setting stones. It is used in conjunction with a form, generally made of wood, that acts as a handle (like a file handle). Work is positioned and released by warming the wax over a soft flame.

Gravers

A graver is used to manipulate metal in the setting process. Gravers are also used for engraving. Gravers are shaped and sharpened using combination sharpening stones, and polished using an Arkansas stone.

Pusher

Use a pusher to manipulate metal onto a stone to set it.

Arkansas stone

BEADING AND STRINGING EQUIPMENT

Beading needles are superfine needles that can be passed through stones or pearls with fine holes. Clear nail varnish is used to fix the knot, so it is less likely to come undone. A sewing needle is used to pull a knot around in the knotting process.

Gimp

Gimp is a fine wire coil used to protect thread from wearing against metal fittings in beading and strings. It is available in a gold and silver color.

13

FURNISHING A BASIC STUDIO

Dental tools

Pusher

Gravers

Gimp

Ring clamp

General studio accessories

The following pieces of useful equipment may already be at hand in the home office or cleaning cupboard.

Magnifying glasses

Adhesive tapes

Glues

Adhesive tapes
Double-sided tape has revolutionized the transferring of patterns for piercing (see pages 22–23), while masking and adhesive tape are useful for tacking down, positioning, and masking out.

Glues
Glues are generally useful to have around as they can be used to tack things together during the making process or for permanent fixing, for example, gluing pearls.

Pencil, permanent marker pen, and eraser
These tools are always useful to have close to hand, for various marking out tasks.

Graph paper
Graph paper is a simple aid for marking out, since work can be placed on it to establish the quarters of a circle.

Scissors and craft knife
Scissors are used frequently for trimming and cutting in general. A craft knife is not just used for trimming and cutting paper, it is also useful for scraping away burrs on metal left from cutting or filing, for example.

Magnifying glasses
For close work, like setting or engraving, magnifying glasses enlarge the work so that detail is more easily visible.

Brass brush
A brass brush is used for general cleaning and can give a gentle sheen to metal. When using a brass brush it is advisable to apply a dishwashing liquid to avoid a deposit of brass being left on the surface of your work.

Furniture wax
Good-quality uncolored furniture wax applied with a soft duster can be used to seal patination (see page 101).

Metal polish
For general polishing and finishing, or for polishing waxes prior to casting into three-dimensional shapes (see pages 72–77), use metal polish on a soft cloth to create a fine finish after wire wool.

Scouring pads
A kitchen scouring pad imparts a satin finish to metal. They can be found in different grades, which affect the range of matte finishes you can achieve with this modest household article.

Soft bristle brush
A soft brush is useful for cleaning when used with dishwashing liquid and warm water after polishing.

Toothbrush
New or old, a toothbrush is a useful tool for cleaning small items such as rings.

Protective gloves and apron
Heavy duty rubber gloves should be worn to protect your hands during a number of tasks, such as pickling and etching (see pages 34 and 92–93), while a heavy apron will offer protection for your clothing during sanding and polishing, and other dirty processes.

Graph paper, marker pen, retractable pencil, and craft knife

Furniture wax

Metal polish

Brass brush

Soft bristle brush

Specialist equipment

The following pieces of equipment have very specific purposes. If you are planning on taking up jewelry-making professionally, and hope to specialize in a few particular techniques, then you may consider investing in these items.

Repoussé bowl and hammer

Taps and dies

RT blanking system gauge

RT blanking system cutting bed

Repoussé bowl punches and hammer

For the repoussé technique (see pages 52–55) you will need a repoussé bowl, punches, and a special repoussé hammer. With this technique, relief can be added to sheet or hollow forms by pushing a variety of punches into flat sheet from the back and front.

Pendant drill

The single most useful piece of equipment beyond your basic toolkit is the pendant drill, also known as the flexible shaft motor. This single unit allows you to drill, polish, grind, and sand, and it can even be used as a limited lathe. It is preferable to operate the speed control by a foot pedal, as both hands will be occupied—one with the work, the other with the tool—making speed adjustment by hand difficult.

Rolling mills

Although a reasonably large expenditure, rolling mills have the advantage of being both a practical and decorative tool. Sheet can be thinned alone, or thinned and decorated using rolling mills (see page 38). If the rollers have square and "D" section grooves as well they can be used to taper or form wire.

Barrel polisher

Barrel polisher

For small-scale production and for polishing chains, the barrel polisher is a clean and efficient piece of equipment that works by tumbling pieces in a soapy solution with polished steel shot—small pellets of metal—that imparts its finish to the work. The polishing media may also be changed so that the barrel can be used for grinding, to clean up casting for example (see pages 74–75).

Taps and dies

Taps and dies are used to make screws and nuts, and are available in an imperial or metric form.

RT blanking system

This is used to make simple steel tooling for blanking, cutting, and repeated sheet forms. The jig is set according to the gauge of steel sheet used for the tooling, so that a shape is cut in the tool at a specific angle.

Large bench vise

For holding larger works or low-relief pressings (see pages 56–57) use a large bench vise screwed onto the bench—a 4 in (10cm) jaw bench vise has adequate strength but must be bench mounted.

Bench press

For pressing (see pages 56–57), consider a manual bench press or hydraulic bench press.

Pendant drill

Rolling mill

Bench press

Materials

The materials most commonly associated with jewelry are silver, gold, and semiprecious and precious stones; base metals and other materials are generally useful for making rough models to test the practicality of your design. Some of the materials more recently introduced to jewelry making, such as titanium and aluminum, cannot be handled in the same way as the precious metals, primarily because they cannot be soldered. Refer to a bullion dealer for metals and stone dealer for stones (see **Bullion and stone suppliers**, pages 124–125). These are a few of the materials that you might come across when making jewelry.

Precious stones are available in a variety of cuts and shapes.

MATERIALS

PRECIOUS METAL
Gold, silver, and platinum are traditionally described as precious metals. These are readily found in sheet, wire, rod, chenier, or as grain for casting into three-dimensional shapes. They are also fashioned commercially into tubes, chains, and fittings and findings. Some bullion dealers will also carry a variety of useful castings of settings and other commonly used forms. The cost of materials varies according to the amount of work undertaken to form it; and a surcharge called the "fashion charge" is added.

Gold
Gold can be found in numerous colors and purity, from 9 karat, as found in the United Kingdom, to 22 karat, which is used more in the Far and Middle East. In general, pure gold is too soft for jewelry purposes. Through the process of alloying, specific characteristics can be achieved such as hardness and color differences. Gold can be alloyed to make yellow, red, white, and green of various hues.

Platinum
This gray-colored inert metal is resistant to tarnishing. It is the most costly of the precious metals, partially due to its relative weight. It is good for stone setting, as it is the hardest of precious materials. Platinum needs high temperatures to solder, and casting it is a specialist job due its high melting temperature of over 2912°F (1600°C).

Platinum

Yellow gold

White gold

Silver

Semiprecious stones come in every color of the rainbow, and are opaque, translucent, or transparent.

Silver
Silver is fairly easy to handle, being a ductile and malleable metal. It is the whitest of the precious metals, although it will tarnish with exposure to air. Sterling silver (marked 925) is alloyed so that it becomes harder than fine silver, but it is less suitable than fine silver for enameling as it contains more contaminants.

PRECIOUS STONES
Precious stones are so named because of their relative rarity. They include diamonds, sapphires, emeralds, and rubies. The highest quality semiprecious stones may actually be more costly than lower quality precious stones.

SEMIPRECIOUS STONES
The semiprecious stones are all stones other than those named as precious. They include pearls, and opaque and transparent stones. Some rare semiprecious stones can be very valuable.

BASE METALS
The term "base" refers to metals that are non-precious, including copper, gilding metal, brass, nickel, steel, aluminum, and titanium.

Copper
Copper is a ductile and malleable pinkish-red metal. It is difficult to

Nickel, brass, gilding
metal, and copper

Shaped wire

Chenier

Aluminum,
titanium,
and steel

Perspex

pierce as it feels "sticky" when worked. It's a useful learning material for soldering as it is forgiving, due to its relatively high melting point of about 1904°F (1040°C)—by comparison to silver's approximate melting point of 1778°F (970°C).

Gilding metal
Gilding metal is a golden-colored metal and an alloy of copper designed for gilding. Its characteristics are similar to silver. It pierces better than copper although is slightly less malleable.

Brass
Brass is a yellow metal, harder than silver, copper, or gilding metal, although not as hard as nickel. Take care when soldering brass, as it has a relatively low melting temperature of about 1715°F (935°C).

Nickel
Nickel is a hard, pale metal with a yellowish tint that oxidizes after soldering, so needs quite a bit of cleaning up. Many people suffer from nickel allergy, so don't use it for ear posts or any other piece likely to sit next to the skin. Nickel is useful for making masters for casting (see pages 70–71) or for model-making. It is

relatively indestructible with a melting point of about 2651°F (1455°C).

Steel
Steel is a gray-colored metal known for its hardness. It is often used for tool-making. Steel comes in a variety of forms including stainless, which avoids the characteristic problem of rusting. Steel oxidizes easily so soldering can be challenging. It needs a different pickle to the precious and base metals already mentioned.

Titanium
Titanium is a hard, light, refractory metal that appears gray. It can be colored through anodizing or by heating, although there is little control when using heat. It isn't possible to solder titanium, so it makes a useful soldering aid as it has a high melting temperature. Titanium is harder than steel and can damage tools such as files and rolling mills.

Aluminum
Aluminum is a lightweight, light gray metal that is soft but sticky to work. It can't be soldered and is a contaminant, so use separate tools.

OTHER MATERIALS
Practically anything can be used for jewelry—from glass and pebbles to "found" objects such as bottle tops and feathers. Each material should be considered for its merits and treated, taking into account its vulnerabilities and durability.

Perspex
Perspex is a good quality hard plastic that comes in a variety of forms. Made from solid sheets and rods, it comes in many different colors, and can be opaque, translucent, or transparent. Perspex can be formed to a certain extent by applying heat, so it is malleable; when cooled it will set into its new form.

Resins
Resins are liquid plastics used for pouring, and so can be cast or embedded. Polyester embedding resin is difficult to handle and

produces unpleasant fumes, so avoid this type. Two-part epoxy resin is a little more costly but is easier to handle and dries tack free.

Wood
Wood is often seen in jewelry as it is relatively easy to carve and adds warmth and color. Always wear a facemask when cutting and sanding wood, to avoid breathing in dust as this can be harmful. Seal, protect, and enhance wood with wax.

Leather and fabric
Leather and fabric are popular for jewelry, as they add color and texture. Consider future cleaning and repair when planning your design. Framing will hide edges that may fray, and will protect the material from body oils.

Fixtures and findings

Measurements and weights:

General data and conversion tables

It is helpful to know certain basic data about materials when considering your options; relative weight can affect function and cost while the melting temperatures may affect your planning of a soldering job. Although the metric system of measurement is commonly used, some people still feel more at home with imperial measures, while others use both forms of measurement in conjunction.

Wire is available in a variety of gauges, so is suitable for knitting or forging.

Composition, melting point, and specific gravity of common metals

Metal	Composition (% of main element/s)	Melting point °F (°C) (approx.)	Specific gravity
Aluminum	100% A	1220 (660)	2.7
Brass	67% Cu, 33% Zn	1715 (935)	8.4
Bronze	90% Cu, 10% Zn	1922 (1050)	8.8
Copper	100% Cu	1981 (1083)	8.9
Gold 24Y	100% Au	1945 (1063)	19.3
Gold 22Y	91.6% Au	1796 (980)	17.7
Gold 18Y	75% Au	1760 (960)	15.5
Gold 14Y	58.5% Au	1598 (870)	13.4
Gold 9Y	37.5% Au	1652 (900)	11.2
Iron	100% Fe	2795 (1535)	7.9
Lead	100% Pb	621 (327)	8.9
Nickel	100% Ni	2651 (1455)	1.4
Silver (fine)	100% Ag	1762 (961)	10.6
Silver (sterling)	92.5% Ag	1688 (920)	10.4
Platinum (fine)	100% Pt	3225 (1774)	21.4
Platinum	95% Pt	3173 (1745)	20.0
Steel (ordinary)	99% Fe	2606 (1430)	7.8
Steel (stainless)	90% Fe	2642 (1450)	7.8
Titanium	100% Ti	3272 (1800)	4.5

Brown and Sharpe gauge to millimeters

Brown and Sharpe is an old-fashioned imperial form of measurements that you may come across.

B and S	mm
4	5.2
6	4.1
8	3.3
10	2.6
12	2.1
14	1.6
16	1.3
18	1.0
20	0.8
22	0.60
24	0.50
26	0.40
28	0.30
30	0.25
32	0.20
34	0.15
36	0.13
38	0.10

Found in limited shapes and sizes, tubing is particularly useful for accurate seam-free settings.

Gem Stone Hardness

Using Mohs' scale of hardness —10 is hardest, I is softest

Stone	Mohs' scale
Amber	2–2.5
Amethyst	7
Andalusite	7–7.5
Aquamarine	7.5–8
Coral	3.5
Diamond	10
Emerald	7.5–8
Garnet	6.5-7.5
Iolite	7–7.5
Jadeite	6.5–7
Jet	3.5
Lapis lazuli	5.5
Malachite	3.5
Moonstone	6–6.5
Opal	5–6.5
Pearl	2.5–3.5
Peridot	6.5–7
Ruby/sapphire	9
Spinel	8
Tanzanite	6
Topaz	8
Tourmaline	7–7.5
Turquoise	6
Zircon	6.5

Separate and store your stones in types to limit damage.

Inch fractions to millimeters

inch	mm	inch	mm	inch	mm
1/16	1.6	1 1/16	27.0	2 1/16	52.4
1/8	3.2	1 1/8	28.6	2 1/8	54.0
3/16	4.8	1 3/16	30.2	2 3/16	55.6
1/4	6.4	1 1/4	31.8	2 1/4	57.2
5/16	7.9	1 5/16	33.3	2 5/16	58.7
3/8	9.5	1 3/8	34.9	2 2-3/8	60.3
7/16	11.1	1 7/16	36.5	2 7/16	61.0
1/2	12.7	1 1/2	38.1	2 1/2	63.5
9/16	14.3	1 9/16	39.7	2 9/16	65.1
5/8	15.9	1 5/8	41.3	2 5/8	66.7
11/16	17.5	1 11/16	42.9	2 11/16	68.3
3/4	19.1	1 3/4	44.5	2 3/4	69.9
13/16	20.6	1 13/16	46.0	2 13/16	71.4
7/8	22.2	1 7/8	47.6	2 7/8	73.0
15/16	23.8	1 15/16	49.2	2 15/16	74.6
1	25.4	2	50.8	3	76.2

Cutting list

When planning a project you will need to make a list of the metals you need, with dimensions, for the process of placing an order. This list is commonly known as a cutting list. If you are ordering precious metal it may be necessary to know the weight of the material to consider if you can afford to proceed without alterations to your design or choice of materials.

Useful information regarding weight

The ounce used to weigh precious metals is known as a troy weight. There are 12 troy ounces to the pound. One troy ounce is approximately equal to 31 grams. The troy ounce is about 10% heavier than the avoirdupois ounce.

Base metals are weighed using the avoirdupois system. There are 16 avoirdupois ounces to the pound. One avoirdupois ounce is roughly equal to 28 grams. The avoirdupois pound is about 21.5% heavier than the troy pound.

Formulae for calculations: computing the weight of sheet, wire, and shot

Weights in grams (g), measurements in millimeters (mm)

Rectangular or square sheet: Length x width x thickness x specific gravity ÷ 1,000 = gram weight

For example, the weight of a piece of 18 carat gold sheet that is 60mm in length, 5mm in width, and 2mm in depth is calculated:

$60 \times 5 \times 2 \times 15.5 \div 1,000 = 9.3g$

Rectangular or square wire: Wire thickness x wire depth x length x specific gravity ÷ 1,000 = gram weight

For example, the weight of a length of square sterling silver wire 4mm square, 200mm in length is calculated:

$4 \times 4 \times 200 \times 10.4 \div 1,000 = 33.28g$

Round wire: This is calculated in the same way as rectangular or square wire, although the calculation must find the circumference of the wire.

1/2 of the diameter, squared, x 3.14 x length x specific gravity ÷ 1,000 = gram weight

For example, the weight of a length of platinum round wire 3mm in diameter, 55mm in length is calculated:

$1.5^2 \times 3.14 \times 55 \times 21.4 \div 1,000 = 8.32g$

Round piece of sheet: 1.2 of the diameter, squared, x 3.14 x thickness x specific gravity ÷ 1,000 = gram weight

For example, the weight of a disc of fine silver 300mm in diameter, 1.5mm in thickness is calculated:

$150^2 \times 3.14 \times 1.5 \times 10.6 \div 1,000 = 1123.34g$

Solid spherical object: 1/2 of the diameter, cubed, x 4.189 x specific gravity ÷ 1,000 = gram weight

For example, the weight of a piece of steel shot 10mm in diameter is calculated:

$5^3 \times 4.189 \times 7.8 \div 1,000 = 32.67g$

jewelry making techniques

While studying jewelry at the Royal College of Art in London, I was fortunate enough to meet some of the leading lights in the field of jewelry. These jewelers were all artists, practitioners, and specialists. No matter where they came from—the United States of America, Australia, Holland, Israel, Japan, or the United Kingdom—they were all exemplary because they had achieved the highest standards in jewelry. And the single most striking impression I gained from watching these jewelers working at the bench was the sense of enjoyment they had for their subject.

Enjoyment is a very important factor in jewelry making, as is quality, and whether it is the simplest piece or the most intricate creation, it takes time, practice, patience, and passion to achieve really good quality results, so you must enjoy the process.

It is hard to reach the zenith in one branch of the discipline, let alone hope to reach such heights across the board. Try as many techniques as you can, then choose those that really excite you to act as the fuel for your passion.

A piece of jewelry is the culmination of many stages of production, so it is important to aim at perfection at every stage. Consider a ring that is made in a dozen stages, and in each stage you have inadvertently created a blemish—that makes twelve blemishes in a single ring!

You will find as you make a piece that you will become intimate with that piece and a strong relationship will often grow between you and your work. At times it will be easy to see faults and be dissatisfied, and yet it may be difficult or impossible to part with this "imperfect" thing.

Making jewelry is a marvellous challenge as it involves diverse skills such as creativity, logic, forward thinking, a good eye, manual dexterity, and even courage. It may be argued that courage is one of the greatest assets in jewelry making since it really can take immense nerve to finish a piece. The closer one gets to finishing, the greater the feeling of risk, as hours of work may be at jeopardy. The feeling of achievement and pride at creating your own jewelry cannot be bought, however, so do persevere.

Piercing

Whether used for complex decorative fretwork or for basic shape cutting, piercing needs to be mastered for accuracy and efficiency.

    The tension of the saw blade is of paramount importance: if a blade is not set properly it will wander, which makes piercing with accuracy almost impossible. To ensure that a pierced image in sheet is the same front and back, the saw blade must be used vertically. If the blade is used at an angle, it is

Simple, round earrings are made three dimensional with a split, a tweak, and a little detailing.

Preparing to pierce

YOU WILL NEED

- Basic hand tools, including piercing saw and 2/0 saw blades (see pages 6–7)
- 2⅜ x 1⁹⁄₁₆ in (60 x 40mm) strip of ½₂ in (0.8mm) thick sheet
- Oil or wax

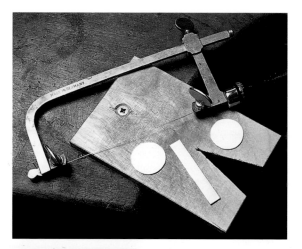

An adjustable saw frame lets you use different lengths of blade and so allows you to carry on using a broken blade, if it is not too short.

A fixed saw frame is easier to tense and more flexible than an adjustable frame.

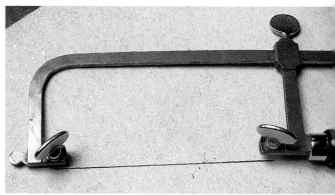

You need to set an adjustable saw frame to the correct length for the length of blade being used.

also more difficult to turn the saw blade to change direction; a vertical saw blade turns by cutting a tiny column-shaped hole, while an angled saw blade cuts a cone-shaped hole.

Saw blades are available in a variety of sizes, from 4—the heaviest—through 0 to 0/6—the finest—which you may choose for particularly detailed fretwork or when working with very thin sheet (see **Saws: frames and blades**, page 6).

Pierced forms are textured and assembled with wire in a pair of brooches.

1 Hold a saw blade against the saw frame with the teeth pointing down to the handle and outward from the frame.

2 Place the blade in the top knuckle and tighten the nut firmly.

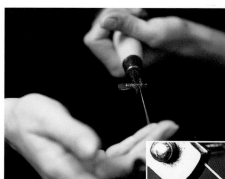

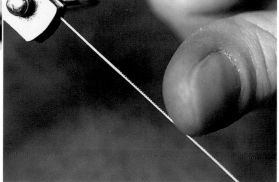

3 Prepare to tense the blade. Sit at the bench and rest the top of the saw frame against the bench peg. Cup the handle of the frame in your secondary hand (your left hand if you are right-handed and vice versa), so that you can push against the bench peg.

4 Lean your body weight on the handle of the saw frame so that the top of the blade is forced upward to the top of the frame. Hold that position, drop the saw blade into the top knuckle, then tighten the knuckle so that it holds the blade in a state of tension.

5 Pluck the saw blade as you would a guitar string, to check the tension. It should make a crisp "ting" sound rather than a "twang." The amount a blade needs to be tensed differs with its weight; a heavy blade such as size 0 would need more pressure exerted than a 2/0. The finest 6/0 saw blade is so fine it can easily be over-tensed.

6 To check that the saw blade is correctly loaded, run your finger up the blade as it faces out of the saw frame. Your finger should "catch" against the teeth. If your finger runs smoothly up the saw blade, it is loaded incorrectly; it may be upside down, facing back into the frame, or both. If it is not loaded correctly take the blade out and start again from step 1.

The cross and gables in this quirky ring are pierced features.

Wax or oil can be used as a lubricant to keep the saw blade running smoothly as both blade and material get hot and "dry" while cutting, causing the blade to break more easily.

Piercing is an essential skill that cannot easily be replaced with mechanical cutting, especially as the scale of the work may be small and forms are often three-dimensional and irregular, making setting up for mechanical cutting impractical. At times, the depth of a line to be cut may exceed the depth of the piercing saw

PIERCING

Piercing a straight line and a circle

There will be many instances where accurate piercing of a straight line will be required, so it is a good idea to try a few practice runs to get you used to this skill. A circle is the most telling curve, since if it is not true the eye can easily detect inaccuracy.

7 To mark out the strip of metal sheet for piercing, set a pair of dividers to ⅜ in (10mm).

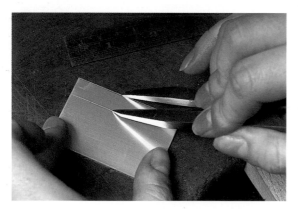

8 Hold one arm of the dividers against the long edge of the metal strip and draw the other arm down to scribe a straight line, parallel ⅜ in (10mm) from the edge.

9 Use the dividers to divide the remaining strip into two squares.

10 Use the dividers to mark the center of the two squares and scribe two 1 in (25mm) diameter circles.

11 Place the sheet on the bench peg so that the line to be cut is over the "V" shaped cutout, but with as much of the sheet as possible braced on the peg. A jeweler's bench usually has a single fixed bench peg with a "V"-shaped cutout for piercing, however, a separate peg that allows the work to be turned and kept horizontal can also be attached. If you are right-handed it should be attached on the left-hand side of the cutout in the bench, and vice versa. Attach the piercing peg with a single countersunk screw centered 1 in (25mm) from the top edge so that it is firmly held, but not so firmly that it cannot turn. A fixed peg can be turned so that the slanted face is used for filing and the flat face for piercing.

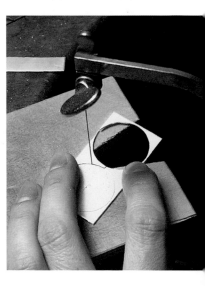

frame, so if you want to pierce long lines or larger forms, you would need to use a deep throated piercing saw. These come in a variety of sizes and are not as easy to handle as a standard piercing saw. This is because the physical balance of the deep throated saw is altered by the extended frame, making it more difficult to control.

Special saw blades are used for cutting wax and Perspex, where the material is inclined to reseal itself as it is pierced due to the heat that is being generated by the cutting action.

Pierced discs are formed to make a hollow pendant detail for a conceptual ring.

12 Hold the sheet with your secondary hand, with your fingers positioned close to the line to be cut. Grip the saw handle lightly in your primary hand so that you can flex your wrist easily to ensure the blade is used vertically.

13 Aim to cut next to the line you have marked rather than on it, so that when you have finished piercing you still have your marked line as a reference for filing (see page 28). To start the cut, run the blade upward on the edge of the sheet at the proposed point of entry.

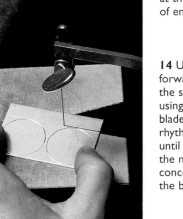

14 Using very little forward force, move the saw up and down using the full length of the blade, keeping a steady rhythm. Continue cutting until you reach the end of the marked line, concentrating on keeping the blade vertical.

15 To pierce a circle you need to cut into the sheet from the edge until you are just outside the scribed line, again leaving the line visible for filing.

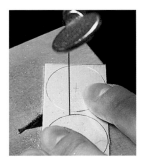

16 You will need to change direction to begin cutting the circle. Without using forward pressure, keep the saw moving up and down on the spot, in a steady rhythm, taking care to keep the blade vertical. Using your secondary hand, turn the sheet by degrees until the blade runs freely. Remember that the blade has a width a tiny bit smaller than its depth, so the amount that it needs to cut to change direction is tiny, and if your blade is vertical a change of direction is quick and the hole made small and neat.

17 Continue cutting the sheet with your secondary hand, turning to pierce the whole circle. Look to where you want to end up to achieve a smooth, flowing line, By forcing the piercing saw into a different direction you will end up with a noticeable change of direction.

18 Repeat steps 15 to 18 to cut the second circle.

Fretwork

Fretwork is the term used to describe perforations in sheet metal that form a pattern of positive and negative shapes. Holes are drilled into the metal to pass a saw blade though, so a negative shape can be cut. There is no simple alternative to piercing, nor is there a simple mechanized method that will do the job as well as piercing, so it is essential to spend time perfecting this skill.

Fretwork takes practice. Be aware that the blade is most easily broken on changes of direction. Thick sheet is more problematic than

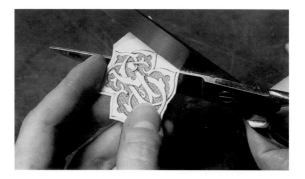

Engraving is used to add further sumptuous detail to a fretwork silver dragon.

YOU WILL NEED

- **Basic hand tools, including piercing saw and 2/0 saw blade (see pages 6–7)**
- **Hand or pendant drill and $^1/_{32}$ in (1mm) diameter twist drill bit**
- **Photocopied cipher or pattern**
- **Pen**
- **Double-sided adhesive tape**
- **Scissors**
- **1$^9/_{16}$ in (40mm) square, according to your cipher size, of $^1/_{16}$ in (2mm) thick sheet**
- **White spirit**
- **Soft cloth**

1 To check that the pattern is suitable for fretwork, color in the negative spaces on a photocopy and see if the positive spaces are still held in position: for example, to cut an "O" you need a tab between the center of the "O" and the rest of the sheet or you will end up with a hole instead of an "O."

2 Photocopy the pattern so that you can keep the original to refer to, adjusting the size on the copier if required.

3 Completely cover the back of the pattern with double-sided adhesive tape, without overlapping the tape and causing raised areas.

4 Trim around the pattern leaving a $^1/_{16}$ in (2mm) border.

5 Remove the tape backing from the paper and stick the pattern close to the edges on the metal sheet, so you don't have far to cut when piercing begins, and to avoid unnecessary waste.

6 Drill a number of access holes (see page 32) inside the shapes to be cut (the shaded areas), about $^1/_{32}$ in (1mm) away from the pattern (the unshaded areas). Position the holes where a line changes direction, such as a corner or the tip of a shape. Avoid positioning a hole halfway along a long, smooth line as you will see clearly the point on the line where you start and finish cutting.

thin, for example. If you do not keep your blade vertical, the pattern will be noticeably different between the top and bottom faces, a discrepancy that will not be as obvious in thin sheet. Turning is also more difficult in thicker sheet if you do not keep your saw blade vertical.

By piercing a fretwork cipher or intricate pattern in relatively thick sheet you can practice turning and piercing a variety of shapes and lines. There are a variety of free patterns suitable for fretwork in specialist "out-of-copyright" books featuring designs and images that can be reused.

Fretwork is used to add subtle detail to a gold and lapis lazuli ring.

27

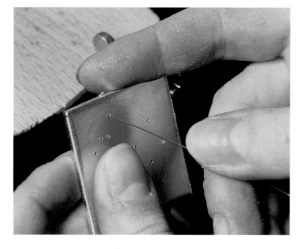

7 Load the saw blade into the bottom knuckle of the saw frame, then pass the saw blade through a hole so the pattern is facing upward in the saw frame.

8 Let the sheet drop to the bottom of the knuckle so that you don't need to support the work. Tense the blade.

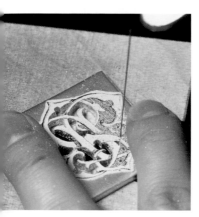

9 Pierce the pattern (see pages 24–25). If you are right-handed, cut in a clockwise direction, so that the pattern is to the right of the saw blade and the line is not obscured by it. If left-handed, cut counterclockwise.

10 If you break a blade, drill another hole nearby rather than passing your blade along the line you have already cut. If your blade becomes stuck, raise the work off the bench peg and let go of the sheet. It will spring into a position where there is no resistance on the saw blade. Reposition the work flat on the peg, hold the saw frame at the new angle, and continue cutting until the shape drops out.

11 Repeat steps 7–9 until you have cut out all the negative shapes.

12 Cut out the exterior shape. To avoid obscuring the pattern with the blade, cut counter-clockwise if you are right-handed and clockwise if left-handed.

13 Peel off the photocopied pattern. Remove residual stickiness with white spirit on a soft cloth in a well-ventilated area, away from naked flames. Sand away any residue using a sanding stick (see pages 82–83).

Filing

Filing removes material by pushing a cutting face over the surface of the metal. It is used to define forms cut by piercing, for thinning the metal wall for a bezel stone setting, to thin or sharpen wire for brooch pins, or to add "shadowing" or low relief on sheet. Files are available in a variety of shapes, sizes, and cuts. The shape of file you choose depends on the job for which it is required. Flat-faced files are used to file straight edges or convex curves, while curved files are used on concave curves. The cut relates to the

A square pendant is filed and sanded to produce crisp lines and perfect form.

Filing straight lines

YOU WILL NEED

- **Basic hand tools (see pages 6–7)**
- **Strip of sheet**
- **Circle of sheet**
- **Wide rectangular section and round section ring**
- **Fretwork strip**

1 To file a straight edge you need to use a flat-faced file. Hold a strip of metal sheet firmly against the bench peg. Place the flat face of the file on the straight edge to be filed. With a downward force, push the file forward, taking care to keep the file level so that you do not file a bevel.

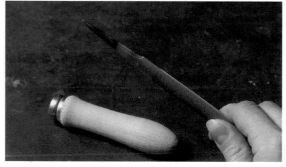

SPECIALIST FILES
Escapement files
Escapement files are tiny specialist files commonly used by watchmakers.
Riffler files
Specialist curved files, called riffler files, are available for filing inaccessible straight or curved areas.

Files should be used with a handle for comfort and safety. To fit a wooden handle, hold the file near the top and heat about 1 in (25mm) of the tang with a soldering torch until it is red hot. Push the file firmly into the wooden handle and repeat until it is firmly in place.

2 At the end of the stroke lift the file off the work. Do not slide the file back to the start position, this is bad practice and inaccurate, since the seesaw action causes a dip at either end of a straight edge.

3 Check the surface and changes in its reflection as it is affected by filing. Decide how to place your file for the next filing action to correct or continue a file mark. It is helpful to have a line marked on your work as a guideline for filing. Check progress against guidelines to establish where you need to file more or less.

amount of material a file will remove and the surface finish it will leave. A relatively coarse cut, a cut 0, is used for the quick removal of material, and will leave a heavily scratched surface. Cut 2 is a good general-purpose cut, it also removes material quickly, and the scratches it leaves are easily removed by sanding. Cuts 4, 5, and 6, also known as polishing files, leave very fine scratches. Specialist Valtitan files can be bought for filing titanium; titanium is harder than steel and thus it will damage ordinary files.

The curves of these hollow earrings are filed to remove any blemishes.

Filing convex curves

1 Use a flat-faced file to file a convex curve. Hold the disk firmly against the bench peg. Place the flat face of the file on the edge of the disk, and, with a downward force, push the file forward with care. Use a sweeping action with the file so that it follows the curve of the line, and concentrate on keeping the file level.

2 Lift the file off the work at the end of each stroke.

3 Check the surface and changes in its reflection as it is affected by filing. Decide how to place your file for the next filing action to correct or continue a file mark. As with filing a straight line, check progress against the guideline.

Filing concave curves

1 To file a concave edge, use a curved file. The half-round file can be too wide to fit into some ring forms, so a narrower file, called a ring file, is used. Hold the ring firmly against the bench peg. Place the curved face of the file inside the ring shank and with a downward force, push the file forward with care, using a sweeping action that follows the curve.

2 Lift the file off the work at the end of each stroke; as with a straight edge, sliding the file back to the start position can cause thinning at the edges of the ring shank.

3 Check the reflection (see step 3, **Filing convex curves**, left).

4 Turn the ring around so that you file from both sides.

Skilled and accurate filing contribute to the precision of this bold ring.

Files will "clog" with use as material is left in the cutting grooves. An easy way to clean a file is to push a metal sheet or copper coin in a diagonal direction across the face—the metal or coin acts as a comb and removes excess material from the grooves.

Filing looks simple, however, it takes practice and concentration to file with accuracy. The best indicator for accuracy is the metal's surface reflection that is produced by the filing process: if the reflection is curved you will know that your line is not straight.

Filing ring shanks

I To file the outside of a wide ring shank, use a flat-faced file. Hold the ring firmly against the bench peg or in your secondary hand. Place the flat face of the file against the surface to be filed. With a downward force, push the file forward with care, keeping the file face flat against the flat face of the ring to avoid thinning the edge.

2 Lift the file off the work at the end of each stroke. Sliding the file back to the start position will also cause thinning at the edge.

3 To file inside a round-section ring use a curved file, either a half-round or a ring file (see **Filing concave curves**, page 29). Hold the ring firmly against the bench peg. Place the curved face of the file inside the ring shank and with a downward force, push the file forward with care, using a sweeping action that follows the curve. You will need to adjust the angle of the file in line with the curvature of the edge of the ring.

4 Lift the file off the work at the end of each stroke.

5 To file the outside of the ring use a flat-faced file. Hold the ring firmly against the bench peg or in your secondary hand. Place the flat face of the file on the surface to be filed, and, with a downward force, push the file forward with care. Use a sweeping action with the file that follows the curve of the line, and concentrate on keeping the file level. Change the angle of the file to account for the curvature of the ring shank.

6 Lift the file off the work at the end of each stroke.

Files used on materials such as aluminum or lead will be contaminated, as material will be left in the fine grooves of the file face and can be deposited into fine metal. Keep a well-marked selection of files for the purpose. Files can be used to work wax, although if they are not cleared frequently they will clog. Remove the wax by warming the file gently with a flame and use a tissue to soak away the melted wax.

Filing is used to finish the fretwork and achieve the perfect fit for the hinge of this locket.

Filing fretwork

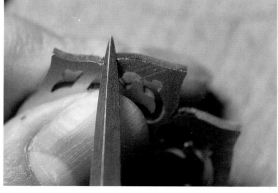

1 Choosing the correct file will depend on the shape of the work to be filed. Use needle files for small spaces and edges, flat-faced for straight edges and convex curves, or curved for concave curves. You may choose to use a barette to get into particularly acute angles, or a square file to achieve a 90° angle.

2 Follow the instructions for **Filing straight lines**, **Filing convex curves**, or **Filing concave curves** (see pages 28–29) depending on the area of fretwork being filed.

3 To file a crease or corner detail, place the file edge into the crease or corner and file away from it. You will not be able to complete the full sweep of the file action if you file toward a corner or crease, and you can cause damage to the area that obstructs the file.

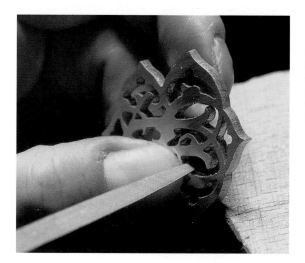

4 Filing internal spaces is difficult, as there is little room for the natural sweep of the file action. An escapement file would be necessary for extra fretwork.

Drilling

Drilling holes for fretwork allows a saw blade to be passed through the metal sheet to access a predefined shape for cutting. Larger holes should be started with a small drill, and worked upward to the size required. Drilling is also used for riveting, so that tube or wire can be passed though a number of sheets or pieces of metal. Holes may also be needed for other decorative reasons: to attach pendants with jump rings, to allow a piece to be hung, or when using

Holes are drilled for rivets and piercing in these layered earrings.

YOU WILL NEED

- **Basic hand tools (see pages 6–7)**
- **Archimedes, bow, or pendant drill and 1/32 in (1mm) diameter twist drill bit**
- **Prepared paper pattern attached to sheet (see Fretwork, pages 26–27)**
- **Wide ring**
- **Pen**
- **Oil or wax**

1 Load a twist drill bit according to the instructions for your drill, ensuring that it is held securely.

2 Mark a point on your pattern inside a shape to be cut, about 1/32 in (1mm) away from the pattern if possible. Mark points on all the areas to be cut.

TIP
A twist drill bit is relatively vulnerable and, if possible, should be loaded so that as much of the shank—the smooth area of the drill bit—is held by the chuck as is possible, without covering the spiral section. When drilling, always hold the work firmly against a solid wood surface. Make sure the work is held level if drilling with a bow or Archimedes drill.

3 The tip of a twist drill bit is pointed, so when presented to a metal sheet it can slip. Make an indentation on each pen mark by pushing the tip of a scriber down hard into the sheet to crease an indent on the point marked.

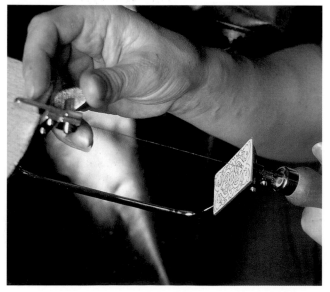

taps and dies to make nuts for a screw fitting.

Drilling a large number of holes by hand can be tedious. A pendant drill is a motorized unit that can be used for drilling. Always wear safety glasses when using a mechanical drill. When drilling large holes, begin with a small hole, then enlarge it by using a slightly larger drill bit each time.

Stone set pendants are attached through holes drilled in the shank of one of a pair of rings.

Layers of detail are attached to the main form through a series of drilled holes.

4 The friction caused by drilling heats up and dries the drill bit and metal sheet. Apply oil or wax to the bit to lubricate it. Lubrication helps to avoid the drill bit getting stuck or breaking—if the bit gets stuck while drilling, the piece can spin out of your grip, which is both alarming and dangerous.

5 When using a hand drill, hold the work firmly on a bench or level bench peg. Position the end of the drill bit in the indentation. Hold the work with one hand while you operate the drill with the other by raising and lowering the movable nut on the Archimedes drill.

6 When using a pendant drill, hold the work firmly against the bench. Position the end of the drill bit in the indentation. Using firm, but not hard, pressure, push the twist drill bit downward to drill the hole. Do not force the drill, which can result in the twist bit breaking. Present the drill bit so that you drill a little at a time, rather than as a single action.

Annealing and pickling

Metal hardens as it is worked or manipulated by processes such as hammering, stretching, twisting, folding, and bending. The more the metal is worked the harder it will become. Metal is heated to a specific temperature to soften it, in a process called

Metal is annealed before forming the pendant and bail in this lavish neckpiece.

YOU WILL NEED

- **Basic hand tools (see pages 6–7)**
- **Soldering equipment (see pages 10–11)**
- **Metal, sheet or 10/11 wire**
- **Silver polishing cloth**

1 Use a soldering mat on the bench to protect it from heat. Prop the metal to be annealed up against a soldering block, or on steel mesh so that heat can circulate easily around it. A turntable, with a soldering block and/or mesh, allows you to rotate the work as you heat it.

Understanding the flame from a soldering torch will help with heating. The hottest point on the flame is at the tip of the inner of the two blue flames, about two-thirds down the length of the whole flame.

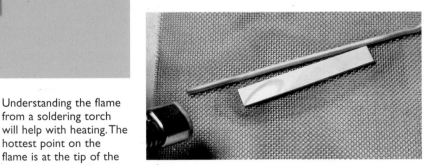

2 Anneal the metal by heating it with a soldering torch. Hold the torch in your secondary hand so your primary hand is free to use other tools. Choose the flame size according to the size of the piece being heated. Avoid using too small a flame. Metal can be heated quickly until it reaches the right temperature (see step 3), then moderate the flame to make sure you don't overheat it.

3 Annealing temperatures differ from one metal to another. As a general rule for gold, silver, copper, gilding metal, nickel, and brass, the metal is annealed when it glows a dull cherry red. Stop heating at this point. Platinum is annealed when it reaches white heat. Since the color of the metal is used as a gauge for when it is annealed, avoid heating under strong lighting or in direct sunlight, where it is difficult to see color changes.

annealing. The metal is then either air cooled or quenched in water before it is pickled, a process that uses a chemical solution to remove the black oxide layer that results from heating. Platinum and pure gold do not oxidize because they are inert metals. The most common pickle for non-ferrous metals is made up of one part sulfuric acid to nine parts water. Specialist commercial solutions can be bought for pickling ferrous metals.

Sheet must be annealed as part of the pressing process for this pendant.

4 Let the metal air-cool for a few seconds. Hold the slightly cooled metal in a pair of tweezers and plunge into a container of water.

In this silver ring, metal will be annealed before it is swaged and formed into a tube.

6 Always use safety glasses and gloves when pickling. Use pickle tongs to place the work in the pickle solution. Leave the work submersed in the solution until the surface is free of oxide, and remove with the tongs. Pickling is quickened with heat; use a small Pyrex dish over a nightlight or an electric slow cooker with ceramic dish and lid .

5 The pickle solutions used to remove oxide from the metals in step 3 are alum (known as safety pickle, alum is mixed with water as per the manufacturer's instructions); or a dilute sulphuric acid solution, one part sulphuric acid to nine parts water (always add acid to cold water when mixing). Do not put steel—such as binding wire—into pickle, as it causes a reaction resulting in copper plating. Steel requires specialist commercial pickling solutions.

7 Rinse the pickled metal well under running water. The dull surface bloom left after pickling can be removed by buffing with a silver polishing cloth.

Doming, swaging, and drawing wire

These are all simple processes for forming metal into specific shapes. Domed forms are made from sheet metal by hammering a punch into an indent with a disc of sheet between them. A swage block is used to make parallel gully or channel forms by hammering a parallel rod into a negative channel.

A necklace of textured and colored domes suggests a constellation of stars.

YOU WILL NEED

- **Basic hand tools (see pages 6-7)**
- **Soldering equipment (see pages 10–11)**
- **Swage block with curved gullies**
- **Smooth metal rods or doming punches to use with the swage block**
- **Round hole draw plate**
- **Doming block**
- **Doming punches**
- **Mallet**
- **Strip of sheet**
- **Bench vise**
- **Oil**

Doming

1 Anneal, pickle, and rinse a circle of sheet metal (see pages 34–35).

2 Choose an indent in the doming block that is larger than the metal circle: if the indent is smaller the circle will be marked by the doming process.

4 Place the annealed metal circle in the indent. Use a mallet to hammer the punch firmly onto the sheet.

3 Choose a punch that is smaller than the indent. Try out different punches in the indent to check that there is space for the metal between the two, to prevent thinning of the edges.

5 Repeat step 4 in smaller indents with the appropriate punch until your dome reaches the required profile.

Swaging

1 Anneal, pickle, and rinse (see pages 34–35) a strip of metal sheet.

2 Choose a channel in the swage block that is wider than your metal strip: if the channel is narrower the edges of the strip will be marked as it is formed.

3 Choose a former, such as a smooth metal rod or a doming punch handle. Check that there is space for the metal between the channel and former, to prevent thinning of the edges.

4 Place the strip in the channel with any overhang at one end only, to limit the marks that may occur.

The swage block is useful for creating relief as well as for raising up strip forms when making tubing. Draw plates are used to make wire smaller, to alter its shape, or make tubes. This is done by "drawing" or pulling the metal through a hole in the plate. Drawing thick wire takes considerable strength and may require a draw bench.

All three processes involve manipulating the metal; it is advisable to anneal frequently so that you are not struggling unnecessarily with work-hardened metal. Overworking the metal will result in split ends and edges.

Silver sheet is swaged to form the curves of this ring that is able to change size.

Drawing wire and tube

1 Anneal, pickle, and rinse (see pages 34–35) the swaged strip (see left).

5 Place the former onto the strip and use a mallet to hammer firmly all along its length.

2 Place a draw plate in a bench vise so that the wider, feed-through holes are at the back. Use tin snips to trim the end of the swaged strip into a "V" shape.

6 Repeat step 4, working on a smaller channel with the appropriate former until your strip reaches the required profile.

3 Use parallel pliers to pinch the "V" into a tight taper.

4 Choose a hole in the draw plate by pushing the taper through from the back so that it protrudes through the other side, but so the strip is just too big to be pulled through.

5 Using heavy, serrated-edge pliers, pull the swaged strip through the draw plate. Use a drop of oil to lubricate the work.

6 Repeat steps 4–5 until the seams of the strip join when pulled though the draw plate.

TIP
For drawing wire, file the end to make a taper (see page 28–31).

Roll milling sheet and wire

The rolling mill is a simple device—similar to a mangle, used for squeezing the water from laundry. Rolling mills for metal have steel rollers, instead of rubber ones, so that they can compress metal as it is passed between them.

Some rolling mills have indents for rolling

Layers of metal—milled with sheet to texture and thin—are used to make a striking neckpiece.

YOU WILL NEED

- **Basic hand tools (see pages 6-7)**
- **Soldering equipment (see pages 10–11)**
- **Rolling mill**
- **Strip of sheet**
- **Circle of sheet or jump ring (see page 42)**
- **Round wire**

Rolling sheet

1 Anneal, pickle, and rinse a strip of sheet (see pages 34–35).

2 To set the width between rollers on a rolling mill, try pushing the sheet between the rollers. If the sheet passes through the gap, turn the handle on top of the mill until the rollers stop the sheet from passing between them.

3 Support the metal in one hand and turn the handle at the side of the mill so that it draws the sheet through the rollers and releases it on the other side.

4 Check the thickness of the sheet using a vernier caliper. If it is still too thick, repeat steps 2–3 until you achieve the required thickness.

Making ovals

1 Anneal, pickle, and rinse a circle of sheet or a jump ring (see pages 34–35).

2 Follow steps 2–3 of **Rolling sheet** (see left) to set the rollers to the required width and feed the disc or jump ring between the rollers.

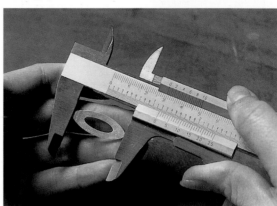

3 Check the thickness or length of the metal shape using a vernier caliper. If it is still too thick, repeat step 2 until you achieve the required thickness.

Feed the circle or jump ring through the rollers in the same direction each time, so that it elongates into an oval form.

wire into squares or "D"-sections. The square grooves are useful for shaping and tapering wire. Milling sheet will elongate the piece, for example a circle can be elongated into an oval form; when halving the thickness you will roughly double the length if rolling a sheet in one direction only.

Rolling sheet and wire involves compressing the metal, which means it will work-harden, so remember to anneal frequently and you will not struggle unnecessarily with hardened metal. Overworking the metal will result in split ends and edges.

Shaping or tapering a wire

The tips of the wires in this neckpiece are milled to add character.

For this technique the rolling mill must have rollers with square grooves.

1 Anneal, pickle, and rinse a length of round wire (see pages 34–35).

2 Push the wire between the rollers in one of the square grooves. There should be no gap between the rollers, unless the wire is larger than the largest groove.

3 Hold the wire in one hand and turn the handle at the side of the mill so that it draws the wire through the grooved section of the rollers and releases it on the other side. If you want to taper the wire, feed a limited section of it through the rollers, rather than allowing it to pass all the way through.

4 Repeat step 3 as necessary, turning the wire 90° each time, to confirm the shape and prevent an unwanted flange that may appear as metal escapes along the rollers.

Forming "D"-shaped wire

For this technique the rolling mill must have "D"-shaped channels on one of the rollers.

1 Anneal, pickle, and rinse a length of round wire (see pages 34–35) .

2 Follow steps 2–3 of **Rolling sheet** (see left) to feed the wire through the "D" shaped section of the rollers.

3 Check the thickness of the shaped wire using a vernier caliper. If it is still too deep in section, repeat step 2 until you achieve the required thickness.

also see the following pages:
Fretwork 26–27 • **Drilling** 32–33
Piercing 22–25 • **Filing** 28–31
Sanding and cleaning up 82–83
Annealing and pickling 34–35
Polishing 84–85

Project 1

Pierced brooch

Piercing sheet metal can leave you with delicate decorative surfaces that are lightweight and practical for jewelry pieces such as brooches and earrings, where weight can, ordinarily, be a problem.

This project shows how the basic piercing and filing techniques can be used to create a piece of jewelry, so you can put the techniques already learned into practice.

YOU WILL NEED

- **Basic hand tools (see pages 6–7)**
- **Soldering equipment (see pages 10–11)**
- **Bangle mandrel**
- **Small mallet**
- **Hand or pendant drill and ½ in (1mm) diameter twist drill bit**
- **Planishing hammer**
- **Steel block**
- **Sanding equipment (see page 80)**
- **White spirit**
- **Soft cloth**

- **Polishing equipment (see page 84)**
- **Double-sided adhesive tape**
- **Scissors**
- **Paper**
- **Pencils**
- **Crayon or color pencil**
- **2⅜₆ x 1¾ in (65 x 45mm) strip of ³⁄₆₄ in (1.2mm) thick sheet**
- **6 in (15cm) length of ³⁄₆₄ in (1.5mm) diameter round wire**

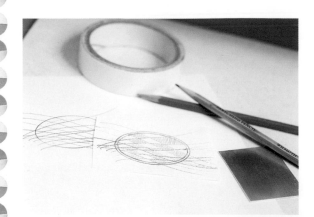

1 Draw an elliptical circle about 2⅜ in (60mm) at the longest point, just smaller than the piece of metal. Draw a second, slightly smaller, elliptical circle inside the first circle to define a border. Draw random diagonal lines crossing each other over the circles.

2 Photocopy the pattern. Color alternate areas between the lines for piercing inside the inner circle. Coloring is a means of defining the pattern for piercing, and limits mistakes when drilling. Cut out the pattern and attach it to a 2⅜₆ x 1¾ in (65 x 45mm) strip of ³⁄₆₄ in (1.2mm) thick sheet using double-sided tape.

3 Drill holes to pass the saw blade through in the colored spaces.

4 Use a piercing saw to pierce the pattern, beginning with the internal spaces, then pierce the outer form.

5 When the piercing is complete, remove the paper pattern. Clean off any stickiness with white spirit on a soft cloth in a well-ventilated area.

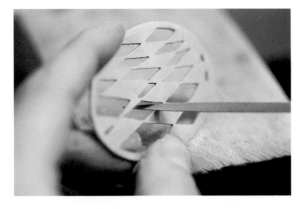

6 Tidy the internal shapes by filing with needle files.

7 Tidy the external form by filing with a hand file.

8 Sand the brooch form using sanding sticks.

9 Anneal, pickle, and rinse the brooch form.

10 Gently curve the brooch by hand over a bangle mandrel, using a small mallet to hammer down any angled areas that remain raised.

11 Sand any blemishes imparted by hammering using sanding sticks.

12 Polish the brooch using polishing sticks and polishing compounds. Hand polish if possible, since polishing with mops on a pendant drill can cause "drag" marks.

13 Anneal, pickle, and rinse a 6 in (15cm) length of ⁄₆₄ in (1.5mm) round wire.

14 Form the wire into a square-sided form using parallel pliers. Hold the wire ⁄₁₆ in (5mm) from one end and bend the first corner. Bend the second corner about ⁄₁₆ in (15mm) from the last. Bend the third corner ⁄₈ in (10mm) from the second corner. Finally, bend the fourth corner ⁄₁₆ in (15mm) from the third.

15 At the point where the straight wire crosses the end of the square-sided form, curve the wire downward to form the pin.

16 Adjust the square so the short end touches the curve of the wire where it drops downward to the pin, as shown above.

17 File the short end to fit the curve of the wire where it drops downward to the pin.

18 File the end of the pin to a taper and a point using a hand file.

19 Form a curve on the pin by hand over the bangle mandrel.

20 Harden the pin by hammering with a planishing hammer on a steel block.

21 Sand and polish the taper and point of the pin.

Forming jump rings

"Jump ring" is the generic term used for simple rings so often used in jewelry. It is important to make uniform jump rings that can be closed with a clean join. This method of making jump rings ensures that each jump ring can be made uniform in shape and size.

The size and function of a jump ring dictates the gauge of wire you use. If it's not going to be soldered, use a heavy-gauge wire that has been hardened. Using two jump rings in conjunction significantly decreases the likelihood that they will come undone.

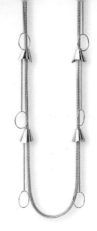

Delicate jump rings are suspended on strands of chain in this necklace.

YOU WILL NEED

- **Basic hand tools (see pages 6-7)**
- **Round wire ⅟₂₅ in (1mm) diameter**
- **Former, such as a metal rod or the shank of a twist drill bit ⅛ in (3mm) in diameter**

1 Hold about 1 in (25 mm) of wire against the bottom of your former and twist the rest of the wire around the former to start a coil.

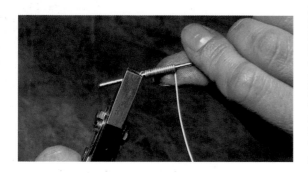

2 It is important to use a downward pressure with your thumb to keep the coil tight. Continue to wrap a close coil around the former until you have as many jump rings as you require. You may want to use parallel pliers or a vise to hold the wire and former.

3 Grip the rings and former lengthwise between your fingers. Hold them firmly against the bench peg and use a piercing saw to cut the jump rings off one at a time, taking care not to cut the former, especially if using a steel former which will blunt the saw blade.

4 To open or close a jump ring, hold it in your secondary hand with flat-nosed parallel pliers and use flat-nosed pliers in your primary hand to twist the jump ring open or closed.

Forming ear hooks and hoops

Earring hooks and hoops can be bought, however they are also easily made. Bought hooks can cheapen the overall look of a pair of earrings, but, with a little time spent with wire, pliers, and formers, hooks can be made to look individual—the icing on the cake rather than a functional extra.

You can use any cylindrical form to make hooks and hoops. Make hooks long enough so that they can't easily be pushed out of the ear accidentally. Hoops should be opened and closed by twisting to the side rather than pulling apart, which will deform the shape point.

Freshwater pearls are added as pendants to finish simple hook and hoop earrings.

YOU WILL NEED

- **Basic hand tools (see pages 6-7)**
- **4 x 2 in (50mm) lengths of ¹⁄₃₂ in (1mm) diameter round wire**
- **³⁄₈ in (10mm) diameter former, such as a metal rod**
- **Steel block**
- **Planishing hammer**
- **¹³⁄₁₆ in (20mm) diameter former, such as a metal rod**

1 Grip the ends of two lengths of round wire with round-nosed pliers and turn them back into small closed loops.

2 Bend the wires by hand around a ³⁄₈ in (10mm) diameter former to make the loop to go through the ear.

Making ear hooks

3 Curve the open wire ends away from the former over a finger to make the hook end.

4 Trim the ends with top cutters if necessary.

5 File (see pages 28–31) the ends to be passed though the ear so there is no sharp point or edge.

6 Hammer the hooks on a steel block using a planishing hammer to flatten and strengthen them.

Making ear hoops

1 Make a coil of wire around a ³⁄₄in (20mm) diameter former by hand.

2 Remove the coil from the former and use round-nosed pliers to turn a closed loop on one end.

3 Use flat-nosed parallel pliers to turn the loop through 90°.

4 Use round-nosed pliers to make a kink at the base of the loop to lower it, so that when the end is cut, it can be secured through it.

5 Cut the hoop off the coil beyond the loop so that the wire can be secured through the loop.

6 Follow steps 5–6 of **Making ear hooks** (see left) to finish. Repeat for second hook.

Forming ring shanks

Rings are one of the most popular forms of jewelry, but they are also one of the most troublesome, due to the size differences of fingers. Whether forming rings from the beginning or altering the size, the process involves moving material with pliers or on a former known as a mandrel or triblet. The width of a ring shank generally affects the size it needs to be to pass over a finger: a wide ring needs to be bigger than a narrow ring to pass over the same knuckle. The vise is integral in this technique as it is used to

In this fanciful ring, the wings are formed from extensions of the ring shank.

YOU WILL NEED

- **Basic hand tools (see pages 6–7)**
- **Soldering equipment (see page 10–11)**
- **Ring mandrel**
- **Bench vise**
- **Large mallet**
- **Small mallet**
- **Ring stick**
- **3⅛ in (80mm) length of ⅛ in (3mm) diameter round wire**
- **3⅛ x ⅜ in (80 x 10mm) strip of ⅟₁₆ in (2mm) thick sheet**

Plain, round silver wire formed into a band makes a simple and wearable ring for daily use.

Forming a round-section ring

1 Anneal, pickle, and rinse (see pages 34–35) a length of round wire.

2 Load the handle of a ring mandrel into a bench vise and tighten firmly.

3 Hold the wire over the mandrel so there is an overhang. Ensuring your hand is firmly braced against the mandrel, use a large mallet to hammer firmly down on the wire beyond the point where it touches the mandrel.

4 Feed another roughly ⅝ in (15mm) section of wire through your fingers and repeat step 3. Continue until the curve of wire is at least ¾ of a circle.

5 Load the mandrel, with the ring form still on it, into the vise, making sure you have fiber grips on the vise jaws to protect

the metal. The unbent length of wire should be pointing upward. Using a small mallet, tap the straight length of wire over the mandrel to continue the curve.

6 Holding the mandrel handle, loosen the vise and feed the ring form around so another straight length can be tapped round if necessary. Your wire should now resemble a tight coil.

7 Remove the coil from the mandrel and check the size with a ring stick. If it is too large, place the coil on its side on the bench and tap the side so that it tightens to the size required.

hold both the metal and mandrel, and it can be used to reduce the strength required for forming.

Metal has resilience and will resist your efforts to bend it, so start bending the metal on a smaller diameter than the size of ring you require. Anneal the ring as you form it, and avoid struggling with work-hardened metal.

The most enduring shape for any ring is the fuss-free band so often seen as a wedding band.

A simple shank is topped with a sprung loaded ball-in-column to alter the size of the ring.

8 If it is too small, place it back on the mandrel and tap the face of the ring so it is forced along the mandrel until it is the size required.

9 Cut off the excess wire with a piercing saw (see pages 22–23).

10 Anneal, pickle, and rinse again.

11 Using pliers, close the ring so the two ends meet and flatten it using a mallet on a steel block.

12 Cut through the join, close the ring as in the last step so both ends meet exactly in line. Repeat this step until there is no gap at the join; the ring is then ready for soldering (see pages 62–63).

Forming a wide ring

1 Follow steps 1–4 of **Forming a round-section ring** (see left) using a strip of sheet, until you end up with a "b" shape. Do not hammer on the straight end over the curled end or you will damage the inside of the ring.

2 If the ends are not in line, put the ring into the vise with fiber grips so half of the ring is held with the join just high of the jaws. Tap the side of the ring with a small mallet until it is in line.

3 Follow step 7 of **Forming a round-section ring** (see left) to size the ring, tapping the top of the curled "b" to make it smaller.

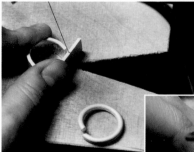

4 Use a piercing saw (see pages 22–23) to cut off the straight end of the strip at the point where it meets the curl.

5 Using pliers, close the ring so the ends meet.

6 Flatten the join by hammering with a mallet on the mandrel.

7 Follow step 12 of **Forming a round-section ring** (see left) to finish.

Forming bangles

Bangles are easy to form in comparison to rings because they are much larger in scale, while the metal used to make them is not significantly thicker than that needed to make a ring. This means that they can be partially formed by hand since the material can be readily bent over a mandrel if it is not excessively wide.

Closed bangle forms, like rings, are subject to sizing problems since hands vary considerably in size. Open bangles address this problem, in

Simple silver bangles are an enduring favorite as they are so easy to live with.

Forming a wire bangle

YOU WILL NEED

- **Basic hand tools (see pages 6–7)**
- **Soldering equipment (see pages 10–11)**
- **Large mallet**
- **Small mallet**
- **Steel block**
- **Bangle mandrel**
- **Bench vise with fiber grips**
- **Sandbag**
- **10 in (25cm) length of ⁵⁄₃₂ in (4mm) diameter round wire**

1 Anneal, pickle, and rinse (see pages 34–35) a length of wire.

2 Load a bangle mandrel into a bench vise with fiber grips and tighten it firmly.

3 Hold the wire over the mandrel so there is an overhang. Ensuring your hand is firmly braced against the mandrel, use a large mallet to hammer firmly down on the wire beyond the point where it touches the mandrel.

4 Feed ⁵⁄₈ in (15mm) sections of wire through your fingers and repeat step 3 to continue curving the wire until it forms at least three-quarters of a circle.

5 Hold the curved section of the part-formed bangle firmly against the mandrel with one hand and use the other hand to pull the other end around the mandrel to create a coil.

6 If the bangle is too large, tighten the coiled wire around the mandrel on a narrower point so it tightens to the size required. If it is too small, force it down the mandrel until it reaches the size required, using a mallet if necessary.

7 To correct any undulation in the form, flatten the form by tapping the face with a small mallet on a steel block supported by a sandbag.

8 Cut through the coil with a piercing saw (see pages 22–23). Keep your fingers out of the center of the coil to avoid cutting them.

9 Anneal, pickle, and rinse.

10 Close the bangle by hand and on the mandrel by hammering both ends at the join with a mallet.

11 Cut through the join again and close the bangle so both ends meet exactly in line. Repeat this step until there is no gap (see pages 44–45).

12 Solder the join (see pages 60–61).

13 Hammer the bangle on the mandrel with a mallet, working small sections at a time to ensure the shape is round. Check the reflection inside the bangle: the areas you have hammered will appear polished, unhammered areas will appear matte.

14 Repeat step 7.

some respects, although you need to make sure that the material used to make an open bangle is suitably robust so that the form is not easily distorted.

When making a bangle you will need to consider the distribution of weight if you intend to include any detailing. The heaviest part of the bangle will be inclined to drop below the wrist unless you consider a counterbalance to right the form.

A single wire is used to circumvent the wrist while wire bangles are held in place by a pressed form.

Forming a sheet bangle

YOU WILL NEED

- **Basic hand tools (see pages 6–7)**
- **Soldering equipment (see pages 10–11)**
- **Bangle mandrel**
- **Bench vise with fiber grips**
- **Sandbag**
- **Large mallet**
- **Small mallet**
- **Steel block**
- **10 x ⅜ in (250 x 10mm) strip of ¹⁄₁₆ in (2mm) thick sheet**

1 Follow steps 1–4 of **Forming a wire bangle** (see left) with a strip of sheet.

2 Position the mandrel vertically in the vise. Hold the curved section firmly against the mandrel with one hand and use the other hand to pull the other end around the mandrel to create a "d" shape.

3 Follow step 6 of **Forming a wire bangle** to size the bangle.

4 Follow steps 7–9 of **Forming a wire bangle**, cutting through at the point where the straight piece meets the curl.

5 Check that the ends of the bangle come together in line. If the bangle is askew, hold it firmly on the mandrel and use a mallet to hammer around the top edge at the end that is pointing up. This tightens the curve so that the hammered end turns downward toward the other end.

6 Cut through the join again and close the bangle so both ends meet exactly in line. To perfect the join repeat this step until there is no gap.

7 Follow steps 12–13 of **Forming a wire bangle**.

Forging and raising

Forging and raising are techniques for reshaping with controlled force. The choice of hammer face, the support's shape, and the skill of the maker will have a direct effect on the material being manipulated. The principle that needs to be understood is what happens to the metal when it is displaced. A cylindrical hammer (curved in one plane) will displace metal at right angles to the curve, while a spherical hammer will displace material evenly all round.

Forging is used with delicacy to create the twisting forms for a lavish organic neckpiece.

YOU WILL NEED

- **Basic hand tools (see pages 6–7)**
- **Soldering equipment (see pages 10–11)**
- **Steel block**
- **Raising hammer**
- **Planishing hammer**
- **Blocking hammer**
- **Bench vise with fiber grips**
- **1³⁄₁₆ in (30mm) diameter doming punch**
- **4 in (100mm) length of ⁵⁄₃₂ in (4mm) diameter copper or silver rod or wire**

1 Anneal, pickle, and rinse (see pages 34–35) a length of rod.

2 Hold the end of the rod (about 1in or 2.5cm) on a steel block and stretch the rest by hammering along the length with a raising hammer. Ensure that the hammer blow is square to the steel block: if the hammer is tilted the rod will begin to curl to one side. If you are using the hammer correctly, the blows should be at 90° to the rod and be consecutive, so that there is no unhammered metal between blows. The section should now be rectangular.

3 Turn the rod through 90° and repeat step 2. The section should now be square.

4 Anneal, pickle, and rinse again.

5 Turn the rod through 90° and continue forging. Reduce the forged area by extending the unforged area to begin a taper.

6 Turn the wire through 90° and forge the rod from the point forged in the last step.

7 Repeat steps 4–6, continuing to reduce the area being forged until the rod tapers to a point.

8 Anneal, pickle, and rinse again. Planish—flatten and polish—the tapered rod using a planishing hammer with the work supported on a steel block. Work along the full length of one forged face of the rod; repeat for the other three forged faces.

A flat support doesn't generally alter the shape beyond the effect of the hammer blow; a cylindrical support will increase the directional effect of a cylindrical-faced hammer if used in the same orientation. Raising is a silversmithing technique for "raising" a flat sheet into a curved, open form such as a bowl.

As a means of understanding the effects of a particular hammer or support, modeling clay is a useful trial material. To work the clay, use the hammers and supports as you would for metal; the clay will be displaced like metal but with little effort.

With simple forging and a little raising, a handsome fibula can be created.

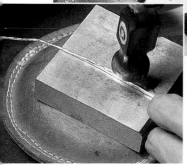

9 Anneal, pickle, and rinse again. Spread the unhammered end section by hammering with a raising hammer over a steel block. Begin hammering the end with the hammer face in line with the rod, tilted slightly downward toward the end. With each hammer blow, change the angle of the hammer so that the far end of the hammer face is radiated in an arc form—the end should fan out, thin, and become wedge-shaped in section.

10 Anneal, pickle, and rinse again. Tidy the join between the tapered rod and fanned detail by hammering with a raising hammer.

11 Curve the detail by raising. Position the fan end over a doming punch and hammer with a blocking hammer in a circular action radiating from the center to the edge.

12 Anneal, pickle, and rinse. Clamp the form on the taper just above the detail in a bench vise with fiber grips. Hold the form about 2 in (5cm) above the vise jaws with parallel pliers. Rotate the form to create a twist. Continue until there are as many twists as desired.

Fold forming

An undulating fibula is made by fold forming and is detailed with creative texturing.

The term fold forming is used to describe any form that has a fold in it, although in this case folded sheet is forged to create extravagant three-dimensional, curvaceous, helix forms. There are some useful traits to forged fold-formed pieces, for example, the forms have no solder seams. Despite their volume, forms are generally light as they are usually made of thin sheet; and the natural structures that result from this technique are remarkably strong and flexible. Due to the organic

YOU WILL NEED

- **Basic hand tools (see pages 6–7)**
- **Soldering equipment (see pages 10–11)**
- **Steel block**
- **Small mallet**
- **Creasing hammer**
- **Bench vise with fiber grips**
- **Blunt knife**
- **4 x 1³⁄₁₆ in (100 x 30mm) strip of ¹⁄₆₄ in (0.4mm) thick sheet**

1 Anneal, pickle, and rinse (see pages 34–35) a strip of sheet.

2 Mark a line down the length of the sheet using dividers set to ⁵⁄₃₂ in (4mm).

3 Place the sheet in a bench vise with fiber grips so the scribed line is level with the top of the jaw of the vise.

4 Bend the sheet at the point of the scribed line by levering it over the vise jaw by hand, then hammering with a mallet to define the fold.

5 Remove the sheet from the vise and complete the fold by bending the sheet by hand.

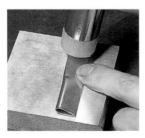

6 Flatten the fold by hammering with a mallet on a steel block, at either end of the fold first then along it.

7 Anneal and pickle again, rinse and dry thoroughly, as liquid is easily trapped in folds. Mark a line on one side of the fold, ⁵⁄₃₂ in (4mm) from the fold, as shown left, using dividers.

8 Place the folded sheet in the bench vise so the scribed line is level with the fold below the jaw.

9 Pry the folded sheet open using a blunt knife.

10 Lever the two sides of the sheet over the vise jaws by hand, then hammer with a mallet to define the folds.

11 Remove the sheet from the vise and complete the new folds by hand.

12 Anneal and pickle again, rinse and dry thoroughly. Use the mallet over the steel block to hammer the new folds as before.

nature of the process, it is almost impossible to dictate a particular curve or to predict the exact length of a piece: an approximation can be made once you are familiar with the process and its outcomes.

Fold forming is suitable for most metals, from precious metals to steel and aluminum. The thickness of the sheet may need to be varied according to the strength and resilience of the metal to be worked: an original thickness of ¹⁄₆₄ in (0.4mm) works well and this process is best explored using copper.

Physically but not visually lightweight, this fold formed silver pendant is both robust and delicate.

13 Using a scriber and steel ruler, mark a tapered line on one side of the folded form, starting the corner at one end to ³⁄₁₆ in (5mm) from the fold at the other. The effect of the taper is to vary the curve of the form: the narrower the form the tighter the resulting curving helix.

15 Use a hand file to clean and level the edge (see pages 28–31).

17 Anneal and pickle again, rinse thoroughly and dry off. Continue to forge the folded form until the curve is to your satisfaction, remembering to anneal the form before hammering an area that has already been hammered since last annealing.

18 Pry the folds of the form open using a blunt knife to begin opening the form, taking care not to scratch it. Once open slightly, continue to pry the form open by hand to achieve a voluminous helix. If necessary, anneal and pickle again, taking care to rinse and to dry thoroughly.

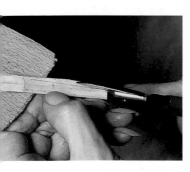

14 Cut along the marked line using tin snips.

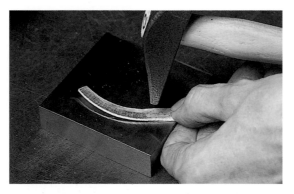

16 Forge (see pages 48–49) along the fold of the form, beginning at the narrow end, using a creasing hammer with the work supported on a steel block. Hammer at 90° to the fold with the hammer face level to the work. Ensure the hammer blows are consecutive with no area left unhammered on the fold between blows. The folded sheet should begin to form into a curve.

Chasing and repoussé

Using chasing and repoussé techniques, sheet is embossed and formed using steel punches. In chasing the steel, tools are hammered into the front of the work, while for repoussé the sheet is worked from the front and the back.

The sheet to be worked is supported in a heavy cast-iron hemispherical bowl filled with a mixture of pitch, plaster of Paris, resin, and tallow that supports the work while retaining enough elasticity to accommodate the movement

Making the pitch mixture

YOU WILL NEED

- **Repoussé bowl**
- **Big old saucepan**
- **Heat source**
- **Stirring implement**
- **16 parts pitch**
- **20 parts plaster of Paris**
- **4 parts resin**
- **1 part tallow**

1 Heat pitch on a stove in a big, old saucepan over low heat until it is molten.

2 Continue heating the pitch, adding the plaster of Paris, a small amount at a time. Mix thoroughly.

3 Without removing the pitch from the heat, add the resin and stir it until it is dissolved.

4 Add the tallow and mix thoroughly.

5 Remove from the heat and pour into the pitch bowl so it is filled to just below the rim.

Chasing and repoussé techniques

YOU WILL NEED

- **Basic hand tools (see pages 6–7)**
- **Soldering equipment (see pages 10–11)**
- **Repoussé punches**
- **Repoussé hammer**
- **Sanding equipment (see page 80)**
- **Brass brush**
- **Dishwashing liquid**
- **Paper template**
- **Double-sided adhesive tape**
- **White spirit**
- **Soft cloth**
- **Old spoon**
- **2 pieces of $\frac{1}{50}$–$\frac{1}{35}$in (0.5–0.7mm) thick sheet**
- **2 pieces of $\frac{1}{32}$in (1mm) thick sheet for the templates**

1 Scrub the $\frac{1}{64}$–$\frac{1}{32}$ in (0.5–0.7mm) thick sheet strips with a brass brush and dishwashing liquid in warm water to remove any surface dirt.

2 Anneal, pickle, and rinse (see pages 34–35) the sheets.

3 Attach a paper template to a strip of $\frac{1}{32}$in (1mm) thick sheet using double-sided adhesive tape.

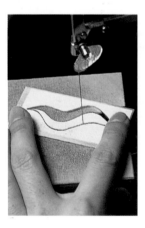

4 Drill a hole near an edge inside the design area and pierce out the negative shape (see pages 26–27). If there is a crease line down your form, as in this example, cut a second template, but only pierce out one half of the motif, leaving the crease line intact.

The undulating form of this ring is formed by the innovative use of chasing and repoussé.

5 Use the two templates to scribe the motif onto the two scrubbed strips of metal sheet.

6 Soften the pitch mixture by warming the surface using a soldering torch with a large, soft flame.

and change in the sheet form as it is struck with the punches. By combining these two processes, relief, hollow, and three-dimensional forms that are lightweight and intricate can be made. Mirror forms are used to make the front and back of a hollow form: if the forms are to have a continuous seam, the shape will have to match exactly, which requires careful and accurate repoussé skills.

There are few techniques that offer such diversity of expression while still being relatively economical on material. It can take some time to create jewelry using the chasing technique,

7 Position the two scribed sheets side-by-side, on the pitch surface, marked side up. If it is warm enough, the sheet will sink slightly so that the pitch begins to enfold the edges. If necessary, carry on warming the pitch with the sheets in place. From now on work both pieces simultaneously.

8 Allow the surface of the pitch mixture to cool completely.

9 Take a repoussé punch that has a gently curved, narrow face, rather like a screwdriver. Hold the punch vertically between

your forefinger and thumb and tap it continuously with a repoussé hammer to chase along the central guideline of each sheet so that you have an unbroken line.

10 Using a narrow oblong punch, emphasize the chased line by working down it as in step 9.

11 Deepen the chased line by working a cushioned (square or rectangle with curved edges) punch, held at a 45° angle to the surface of the sheet, along the form either side of the chased line.

12 Warm the pitch mixture with a soldering torch, then lever and lift out the sheets using tweezers.

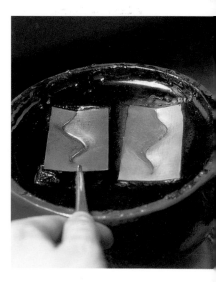

although with practice, complex and delicate pieces can be made, which would be virtually impossible to complete using any other method.

Repoussé is a process that takes a considerable amount of time, as it involves repeating a number of time-consuming stages: the preparation of a sheet by annealing; cleaning to remove the pitch between annealing and work; setting up; and careful work with punches.

Crisp and curvaceous, the lines of this repoussé brooch are clean, precise, and eminently tactile.

13 Clean off excess pitch with white spirit and a soft cloth.

14 Anneal, pickle, and rinse the two chased sheets. Invert the sheets and scribe guidelines for the outline of the forms using the main template.

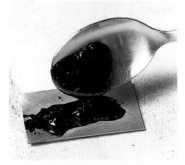

15 Spoon a small amount of warmed pitch mixture into the inverted forms.

16 Allow the pitch to set, then follow steps 6–7 to position the sheets, filled face down, in the pitch bowl.

17 Define the outline of the form by chasing along the guidelines with the punch used in step 9, as shown above.

18 Release and remove the pieces from warmed pitch. Remove the pitch from inside the shapes and clean off excess with mineral spirits. Invert the forms again and reposition them in the warmed pitch mix.

19 Flatten the edges of the forms by working along the faces with a flat-faced punch to produce a shallow "V" section. Hold the punch against the area to be worked at an angle so the sides of the form become as flat as possible.

20 Flatten the area around the inverted form by working over the entire sheet beyond the defined form using a flat-faced punch held vertically.

Punches for chasing and repoussé can be bought in a variety of shapes and sizes, but the quality of bought punches can vary. Punches can also be made from steel, and customized.

Consider putting time aside to explore and refine this technique, rather than expecting perfection first time around, or you may end up feeling frustrated.

Twinned silver wire is used to complete these simple yet eyecatching earrings.

21 Remove and clean the forms.

22 Anneal, pickle, and rinse the forms and fill with pitch mixture. Allow the pitch in the forms to set before positioning them, filled face down, in the pitch bowl.

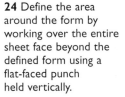

24 Define the area around the form by working over the entire sheet face beyond the defined form using a flat-faced punch held vertically.

23 Flatten the sides of the form using a flat-faced punch held against the area to be worked at an angle so the sides of the form become as flat as possible.

25 Clean the faces of the form by sanding by hand (see pages 80–81). Remove the formed sheets and clean as before.

26 Cut out the forms using a piercing saw and finish by filing the edges (see pages 28–31) and sanding and polishing as required.

Pressing

Pressing is a means of creating three-dimensional forms from sheet by pressing a positive form into a negative space with a piece of sheet held between the two. The method described here can be achieved with a large bench vise tightened manually, however, this takes some considerable strength so the material thickness is restricted to the strength of the jewelry-maker and of the vise. A manual press, as used in the dental industry, is a relatively small, low-cost, low-tech press that gives more compression strength than a bench vise, although a

A hollow pendulous form completes a striking feature in a neckpiece.

YOU WILL NEED

- **Basic hand tools (see pages 6–7)**
- **Planishing hammer**
- **Steel block**
- **Wax saw blade**
- **Wax rasp**
- **Bench vise**
- **Large bench vise**
- **Scissors**
- **Pen (optional)**
- **Masking tape**
- **¹⁄₁₆ in (1.5mm) thick sheet for the former**
- **¹⁄₆₄ in (0.4mm) thick sheet for pressing**
- **⅛ in (4mm) thick Perspex sheet**
- **Rubber sheeting**

1 Mark the shape to be pressed on the metal sheet former using a scriber, drill an access hole, and pierce out the shape (see pages 24–25).

2 File the inside edge of the cutout (see pages 30–31).

3 Mark the same shape on the Perspex sheet, using the metal former as a template. If your shape is asymmetrical and you want to have a pressing

for the front and the back, you will need to use the sheet former as a template for the front and the back of the Perspex. Mark your metal former as having a side A and side B. Mark the Perspex likewise. Ensure that the metal former is central when used as a template for marking so that the cutout is correctly positioned; this allows you to use the same tooling for both pressings.

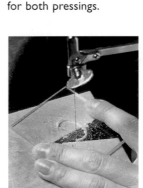

4 Drill an access hole and pierce the Perspex shape using a wax saw blade.

5 File the cutout using a wax rasp to remove material quickly, followed by a hand file for refining.

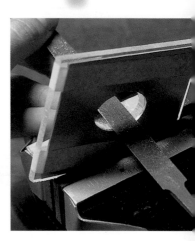

6 Position the metal and Perspex formers together and align the cutouts. Secure with masking tape. Holding the two in a vise, use a hand file to file the cutouts so that they match.

7 Anneal, pickle, and rinse the sheet metal for pressing (see pages 56–57).

hydraulic press will have considerably more compression power so larger pressings can be made using thicker metal.

The Perspex supports the sheet former, which is used to define the edge and keep the form crisp. If you want a particularly deep pressing you will need to use a thicker Perspex former. If tooling is well made it will last well and make precise forms.

An unembellished silver cushion form makes a simple and tactile pendant.

8 Position the pressing sheet over the former—ensuring it is centered over the cutout—and fix with masking tape.

9 Top the former and pressing sheet with some rubber sheeting followed by a steel block.

12 If the pressing is still not deep enough, remove the pressing sheet from the former, anneal, pickle, rinse, and repeat steps 10–12.

13 If a pucker of metal forms, leave the pressing sheet fixed to the former and hammer the puckered area using a planishing hammer on a steel block.

11 Remove the stack from the vise and lift off the steel block and rubber sheeting. Cut a new piece of rubber sheeting to match the cutout shape. Place the new cutout over the indent made by the first pressing, and re-form the stack. Press in the vise again.

14 Release the pressed form from the former.

15 If you are pressing an asymmetrical form, repeat steps 5–15 on side B of the metal and Perspex former.

10 Place the stack in a large bench vise and tighten, using significant force.

Blanking

Blanking using a die is a low-tech system for making multiple reproductions of identical sheet forms. Blanking was developed from an industrial process used in the aircraft industry in the 1930s and 40s.

A design is cut—with a single cut—into a steel sheet that forms the die plate. The sheet to be blanked is inserted into the die plate and hammered between two steel blocks with a heavy mallet. The design is connected to the die by a hinge or tab, so the die is

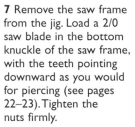

The familiar lines of a jigsaw are cut by blanking before being formed into a ring.

YOU WILL NEED

- **Basic hand tools (see pages 6–7)**
- **RT blanking system**
- **Hand or pendant drill and ¹⁄₁₆ in (2mm) diameter twist drill bit**
- **2 steel blocks**
- **Large mallet**
- **3¼ x 3 in (80 x 75mm) piece of ¹⁄₃₂ in (1mm) thick steel sheet for the die**
- **6 x 2¾ in (150 x 70mm) piece of ³⁄₆₄ in (0.5mm) thick sheet for blanking**

1 Scribe a central line down the length of the steel sheet.

2 Scribe parallel lines ³⁄₁₆ in (5mm) either side of the central line.

3 Scribe two lines at 90° to the central line, one ³⁄₈ in (10mm) from the edge, the other ¾ in (20mm) from the edge.

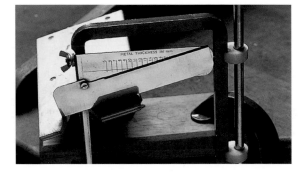

4 Draw a simple design, no larger than 1½ x 1 in (40 x 25mm) on the steel sheet so that the base of your design lies on the last line scribed.

5 Drill ¹⁄₁₆ in (2mm) diameter holes (see pages 32–33), one on each point of intersection between the parallel lines scribed in step 2 and the first line scribed in step 3.

6 Set the angle of the sawing table on an RT blanking system as the manufacturer instructs, using the gauge provided (above). If you are right-handed, the sawing table should slant down to the left, if left-handed it should slant down to the right. The angle at which the table is set will depend on the steel sheet you are using to make your die; in this case it should be ¹⁄₃₂ in (1mm) thick.

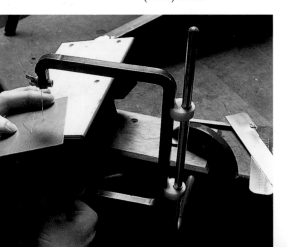

7 Remove the saw frame from the jig. Load a 2/0 saw blade in the bottom knuckle of the saw frame, with the teeth pointing downward as you would for piercing (see pages 22–23). Tighten the nuts firmly.

8 If you are right-handed, pass the blade through the right-hand hole drilled in the steel sheet from the back. If you are left-handed, use the left hole.

9 Allow the steel sheet to drop to the base of the saw blade so that you can tighten the top nut. Tighten the blade as described in the manufacturer's instructions.

10 Attach the saw frame to the jig with the steel sheet resting on the sawing table.

11 Cut the design by piercing along the scribed line until you reach the drilled second hole. Release the die from the saw frame.

self-aligning: a tab will also be left on the blanked sheet and this can be trimmed off or incorporated into the design. The thickness of the sheet to be blanked determines the thickness of the sheet used for the die. The die should be at least as thick as the metal to be blanked.

The RT blanking system was developed and patented in the 1970s by Roger Taylor of the U.K. In the U.S., in the 1980s, David Shelton refined and developed blanking dies to be used with a hydraulic press. Both systems are available for purchase (see **Suppliers**, pages 124–125).

Lightweight sheet shapes can be manipulated to make simple relief forms suitable for earrings.

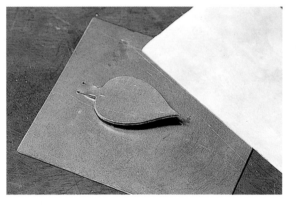

12 Push the design down from the top face so there is a gap into which you can feed the sheet to be blanked.

13 Anneal, pickle, and rinse (see pages 34–35) the sheet to be blanked.

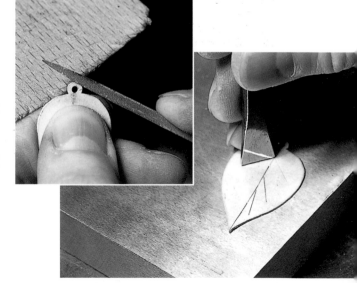

15 To cut the sheet, place the die and sheet between two steel blocks and strike the stack hard with a large, heavy mallet to blank a form.

16 Repeat steps 14–15 to blank further forms. Consider the positioning of the sheet to avoid unnecessary waste.

14 Place the annealed sheet in the die so the edge is beyond the design and in the tab area.

17 You can trim and finish the tab area by drilling, piercing, and filing (see pages 28–31), if appropriate.

also see the following pages:
Annealing and pickling 34–35
Piercing 22–25 • **Fold forming** 50–51
Forging and raising 48–49
Forming ear hooks and hoops 43
Polishing 84–85

Project 2

Fold-formed earrings

Fold forming involves minimal equipment and just a few skills, while the resulting forms are both visually appealing and technically intriguing. It is an ideal technique for elaborate earrings, as forms can be made that are quite large yet still light.

60

FOLD-FORMED EARRINGS

YOU WILL NEED

- **Basic hand tools** (see pages 6–7)
- **Soldering equipment** (see pages 10–11)
- **Bench vise with fiber grips**
- **Creasing hammer**
- **Small mallet**
- **Steel block**
- **Blunt knife**
- **¹³⁄₁₆ in (20mm) diameter former**
- **Planishing hammer**

- **Oxidizing equipment** (see page 87)
- **Polishing equipment** (see page 84)
- **2⅜ x ¹³⁄₁₆ in (60 x 20mm) piece of ¹⁄₆₄ in (0.4mm) thick sheet**
- **¹⁄₃₂ in (0.9mm) diameter round wire**

1 Anneal, pickle, and rinse a 2⅜ x ¹³⁄₁₆ in (60 x 20mm) strip of ¹⁄₆₄ in (0.4mm) thick sheet.

2 Pierce the sheet in half to make two 1³⁄₁₆ x ¹³⁄₁₆ in (30 x 20mm) pieces.

3 Mark a line down the center of each sheet using dividers set to ⁹⁄₁₆ in (15mm).

4 Place one of the sheets in a bench vise with fiber grips so the line is level with the top of the jaw of the vise. Bend the sheet at the point of the marked line by levering it over the vise jaw by hand. Hammer the fold with a mallet to define it.

5 Remove the metal from the vise and complete the fold by hand. Flatten the form by hammering with a mallet over a steel block.

6 Using dividers, mark a line ⅛ in (3mm) from the folded edge.

7 Place the sheet in the vise so the new scribed line is level with the jaw, then prize the folded sheet open using a blunt knife.

8 Lever the two sides of the sheet over the vise jaws by hand, then hammer with a mallet to define the folds.

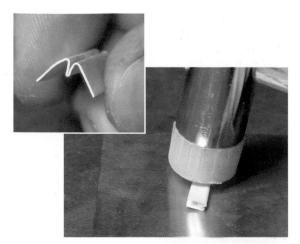

9 Anneal, pickle, and rinse again, then complete the fold by hand and flatten by hammering with a mallet over a steel block.

10 Using a scriber and steel ruler, mark a tapered line on one side of the folded form, starting at one corner, from the fold at one end, to ⁵⁄₃₂ in (4mm) from the fold at the other end.

11 Cut along the marked line using tin snips.

12 Anneal, pickle, rinse, and dry thoroughly. Then, using a creasing hammer on a steel block, forge along the folded edge beginning at the narrow end of the form. Hammer at 90° to the fold with the hammer face level with the work. Ensure there is no area left unhammered on the folded edge. The sheet will begin to form a curve.

13 Continue hammering the folded sheet into a semicircle, remembering to anneal, pickle, rinse and dry the form thoroughly whenever it becomes hard to hammer.

14 Anneal, pickle, rinse, and dry the curved metal. Begin to prize the center fold and the sides at one end of the form open using a blunt knife, taking care not to scratch the form. Continue prizing the form open along the rest of the center line.

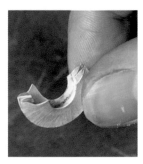

15 Prize the form open by hand until it is the shape required.

16 Repeat steps 4–15 with the second strip of sheet, this time forging on the opposite side of the fold.

17 Use ¹⁄₃₂ in (0.9mm) round wire to make a pair of ear hoops. Don't cut the hoops too short, but test the fit of the hoop and the form and adjust if necessary. Hammer the hoops with a planishing hammer over a steel block to strengthen them.

18 Use a pendant drill with mops and polishing compounds to polish the forms.

19 Assemble the forms and the hoops, as shown below.

Soldering simple joints

Soldering is heating two metals with a more fusible alloy, called a "solder," binding them together. Solder joints are more secure if there is a sizable contact area. Silver solder is used to join base metals as well as silver. Gold solders need to be matched for fineness (9, 14, 18, or 22 carat) and color (yellow, white, or red). Solders can be bought in various melting temperatures from easy (low temperature) to hard (high temperature). Platinum needs extremely high temperatures for

A bold silver ring with bar detail soldered on a simple ring shank.

YOU WILL NEED

- **Basic hand tools (see pages 6–7)**
- **Soldering equipment (see pages 10–11)**
- **Hard silver solder**
- **Ring (see pages 40–41)**
- **Very small jump ring**
- **Earring**
- **¹⁄₃₂ in (0.9 mm) diameter round wire**

Soldering a ring shank

1 Rub a flux cone against the base of a flux dish with a little water until you have a creamy mixture: watery flux is not effective.

2 Using tin snips, fringe the hard solder then cut off "pallions" into a suitable container. The amount of solder required varies according to the size of the join. For a small join like this, two or three ¹⁄₃₂ in (1mm) square pallions, about ¹⁄₆₄ in (0.5mm) thick should do.

3 On a soldering mat, set up the ring on a soldering block over steel mesh, with the join facing upward.

4 Use a flux brush to paint the prepared flux onto the join.

5 Warm the flux with a soldering torch until it stops bubbling: pallions of solder will be displaced by bubbling flux.

6 Use brass tweezers to place pallions of solder on the join. When positioning, bear in mind that solder is drawn to heat.

soldering. Specialist solders are also available that can withstand the temperatures required for enamelling.

Flux is the generic name for an antioxidant used in the soldering process to abate oxidization caused by heating metal. Flux must be removed by pickling; old flux becomes a barrier once the antioxidant chemicals have been burnt off and is harder than steel, so will damage files and blades. Setting up soldering jobs is the key to success: soldering is easier if the work is supported so it can't move. Use the soldering torch in your secondary hand so your primary hand is free to operate tools. Anneal a "worked" piece before soldering.

Simple hoop earrings where the soldered post is an integral detail.

7 Heat the ring from the back, working the heat forward to the join. Take the piece to temperature swiftly, until it glows bright orange. Once you have reached temperature, soften the flame to stop raising the temperature so quickly, which could melt the piece.

8 Continue gently heating, taking care to heat the two sides of the join evenly, until the solder becomes molten and flows into the join. Stop heating. If one side becomes hotter than the other the solder is likely to jump to that side as it melts. If this happens, use a solder probe to tease it back across the join.

9 Allow the work to cool for a few seconds, then quench in water (see step 4, page 34)

10 Pickle (see steps 5–6, page 35) until all the flux is removed, remembering that flux takes longer to remove than oxide.

11 Rinse the work in cold water.

12 If the join has any gaps, repeat steps 3–11, adding a little more solder if necessary. If the gap is due to the solder not having run completely, you do not need to add more solder, just flux again, and heat the piece for longer.

Soldering an earpost

1 Follow steps 1–8 of **Soldering a ring shank** (see left) to solder a small jump ring to an earring back.

2 Position round wire in the jump ring using sprung tweezers.

3 Follow steps 8–11 of **Soldering a ring shank** (see left).

Soldering a hollow form

Soldering hollow forms can be problematic, because liquid can become trapped within the form. Liquid becomes steam on heating, causing a build-up of pressure within the form, which can cause it to explode. If a partially joined piece is to be heated a second time, ensure that there are air vents large enough to allow liquid to be released as steam. This is also useful when it comes to rinsing after pickling; if possible, there should be a minimum of two vents positioned diametrically opposite each other, near or on an edge,

A hollow formed pendant is made to echo the hollow at the base of the neck.

YOU WILL NEED

- **Basic hand tools (see pages 6–7)**
- **Soldering equipment (see pages 10–11)**
- **Hard silver solder**
- **Coarse sandpaper**
- **Glass or Perspex to sand on**
- **Pin hammer**
- **Pins**
- **2 hollow sheet metal shapes, such as those made in Pressing (see pages 56–57)**

1 Anneal, pickle, and rinse (see pages 32–33) two hollow sheet forms. This ensures there is no tension left in the pieces from pressing.

2 Pierce out the shapes to be soldered (see pages 24–25).

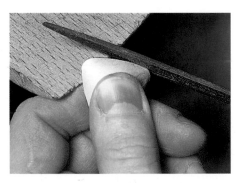

3 File the shapes' edges (see pages 28–29). File the form so there is no flat sheet left.

4 Sand (see page 82–83) the shapes until you have a perfect fit between the two. There should be no gaps.

5 Prepare the flux and paint it onto the seam of the top piece (see steps 1 and 4, page 62).

6 On a soldering mat, set up the fluxed form tilted against a soldering block on steel mesh. Using tin snips, fringe the solder into pallions of about $\frac{1}{16} \times \frac{1}{8} \times \frac{1}{64}$ in (2 x 4 x 0.5mm). Use brass tweezers to position a pallion just in from the seam.

7 Heat the solder until it partially melts, without running. This is known as "sweat" soldering and it secures the solder so it can't move unexpectedly.

8 Repeat steps 6–7 to position three more evenly spaced pallions.

9 Pickle and rinse, making sure all the old flux is removed.

10 Place the second form on the soldering block, seam facing upward, and hammer pins in tightly to keep it in place.

to allow the exchange between air and liquid within the form. Air vents need not be drilled holes; consider this element as part of the overall design.

Joining hollow forms allows you to make lightweight, three-dimensional shapes. Hollow pieces that are not backed can look tinny, while flat-plate backs on curved forms can look harsh—a curved back is tactile and visually satisfying.

Hollow doughnut shapes are used to make large but lightweight earrings.

11 Paint flux onto the seam.

12 Flux the seam of the top piece and place the two pieces together.

13 Heat the join gently with a soldering torch. The forms may move as the flux bubbles, so use a soldering probe to reposition them if necessary, until the flux settles. Do not stop heating while you reposition the pieces as the flux will set if cooled.

14 Heat the forms evenly until the solder runs across the seam: bear in mind that the top form will act like an umbrella shading the bottom form from the heat.

15 Allow the work to cool for a few seconds, then quench in water.

16 Pickle and rinse.

17 Check the seam for gaps. Areas of the seam that are not soldered will trap flux that is burnt out, which acts like a barrier, while liquid can also get in through small holes and become trapped. If there are gaps, you will need to resolder the piece. To avoid an explosion on resoldering, drill (see pages 32–33) two holes in your piece at diametrically opposite points near or on the seam. Flux the seam and add small pallions of solder to the gaps. Follow steps 15–17.

19 File (see pages 26–29) the seam to finish.

Bezel stone setting

The bezel, or rub-over, setting consists of a wall of metal that is pushed over a supported stone to stop the stone from dropping out. The height of the bezel—the wall of metal—required for setting is dictated by the proportions of the stone. For a cabochon stone, the top of the setting wall needs to extend up the stone to a point that is smaller in section to that of the base, so that when the wall is pushed over it will hold the stone in. If the wall is too high you will see too much setting and too little stone. For a cut stone, the height of the

A number of stones are bezel-set around the shank of this gold ring.

BEZEL STONE SETTING

YOU WILL NEED

- **Basic hand tools** (see pages 6–7)
- **Soldering equipment** (see pages 10–11)
- **Hard solder**
- **Setting equipment** (see page 13)
- **Small mallet**
- **Ring mandrel**
- **Planishing hammer** (optional)
- **Steel block**
- **Coarse sanding paper** (see page 80)
- **Sheet of glass, minimum** ³⁄₁₆ **in (5mm) thick with sanded edges**
- **Piece of** ¹⁄₃₂ **in (0.8mm) thick sheet, larger than the formed bezel, for the base plate**
- **Piece of** ¹⁄₆₄ **in (0.4mm) thick sheet for the bezel**
- **Oval cabochon stone**

1 Establish the height of the bezel using dividers. Place one arm at the base of the stone and set the other to a point over the curve of the stone. Measure the diameter of the stone by wrapping a strip of paper around it, and adding a little extra.

2 Pierce a strip of ¹⁄₆₄ in (0.4mm) sheet (see pages 22–25) to match the measurements taken in step 1.

3 Anneal, pickle, and rinse the strip (see pages 34–35).

4 Wrap the strip around the stone and pierce off the excess sheet.

5 Prepare the join (see pages 44–45).

6 Solder the bezel using hard solder (see pages 60–61).

7 Hammer the bezel circular using a mallet and a ring mandrel (see pages 44–45).

8 Using parallel pliers, squeeze the setting into an oval to fit the stone. If the setting is too small, stretch it by hammering small sections at a time on the ring mandrel with a planishing hammer. If the setting is too big, cut out a section and repeat steps 5–7.

9 Sand (see pages 80–81) the base of the bezel on a piece of coarse sanding paper supported by a sheet of glass to keep the paper level.

10 Flux the base plate and position the bezel on it, evenly spacing pallions of hard solder around the outside of the bezel. Solder the bezel to the base plate.

wall tends to be less varied as even a large stone has a relatively small dimension between girdle and table. An easy way to estimate the length of metal needed for a setting is to wrap a strip of paper around the stone and add a little extra to account for the thickness of the sheet.

To set a faceted stone or give depth to the setting for a cabochon stone you can create a ledge, or "bearer," on which the stone can rest.

Pearls set in rub-over settings are the center detail in a pair of ornate gold earrings.

11 Pierce out the base plate around the bezel.

12 File (see pages 28–31) and sand the bezel so that you can no longer see the solder seam.

13 Using dividers, mark a ⅛ in (3mm) wide center bar inside the setting. Pierce out the spaces around the bar.

14 File the edges of the bar with a needle file.

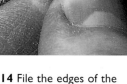

15 Prepare a setter's stick by warming setter's wax over a soft flame and building it up on a file handle or other suitable piece of wood. Shape the wax by rolling it, while malleable, on a steel block.

16 Embed the bezel in the warm wax so that the top is exposed, then allow the wax to cool.

17 Position the stone in the setting, holding the setter's stick firmly against the bench peg with your fingers underneath the peg.

Lapis lazuli is set in a rub-over setting to make a simple, pleasing pendant.

18 Brace your thumbs against the setter's stick, holding a pusher against the top edge of the bezel. Lever your arm upward with a firm, forward pressure to push the bezel over the stone.

19 Repeat on the opposite side of the bezel, then work methodically all the way around the setting until there are no gaps between stone and bezel.

20 Warm the wax over a soft flame and lever the setting out from the softened wax. Remove excess wax with acetone.

Claw stone setting

Claw settings are popular as they allow light to reach the stone and offer fairly easy access to the stone for cleaning. The relatively small amount of material that is used to hold the stone in place means that claw settings are more vulnerable than bezel settings. Gold rings were often made with platinum settings since platinum is a stronger metal. The number of prongs or claws in a setting is a matter of

A claw set diamond is suspended between the arms of a simple tapered ring shank.

YOU WILL NEED

- **Basic hand tools (see pages 6–7)**
- **Soldering equipment (see pages 10–11)**
- **Hard solder**
- **Setting tools (see page 12)**
- **Small round mandrel**
- **Small mallet**
- **Graph paper**
- **6 in (15cm) length of ³⁄₆₄ in (1.2mm) diameter round wire**
- **⁷⁄₁₆ in (11mm) diameter faceted stone**

1 Anneal, pickle, and rinse (see pages 34–35) a length of wire.

2 Using a small round mandrel or other appropriate former, make two jump rings (see page 40), one with a ⁹⁄₃₂ in (7mm) inside diameter, the other with a ¹¹⁄₃₂ in (9mm) inside diameter.

3 File the ends of the jump rings if necessary (see pages 28–31) and close them so that they lie flat.

4 Solder both jump rings using hard solder (see pages 62–63).

5 Using a Cut 2 round needle file, file two round grooves diametrically opposite each other on the edge of both jump rings: use graph paper as an aid to mark the grooves accurately.

6 Hold a 1⅝ in (4cm) length of wire in the center with ring- or round-nosed pliers and bend the two sides up into a splayed "U" to make the prongs of the setting.

7 Push the smaller jump ring down into the "U" wire so the prongs locate in the grooves.

8 Position the larger jump ring between the prongs in the same way with a gap of about ⅛ in (3mm) between the two jump rings. Make sure the jump rings are sitting level between the prongs and adjust the angle of the "U" form if necessary using ring- or round-nosed pliers.

9 Apply flux and hard solder to each join area and solder the structure together.

10 Mark the position for the remaining prongs on the quarters of both jump rings using dividers: use graph paper as an aid to set the dividers.

personal choice—as few as three is sufficient—as long as the stone is held securely in place. The prongs should be checked regularly; even though they may look intact from the top, the wear is generally to the side of the claw at the point where it rounds the girdle, as this is where prongs are likely to receive the most knocks and abrasions.

A single diamond is held aloft in a claw-set platinum ring.

11 File grooves on both rings where marked as in step 6.

12 Solder an ⁵⁄₁₆ in (8mm) length of wire laid across the two jump rings in the first pair of grooves.

13 Repeat step 12 to solder a fourth prong.

14 Cut off the bottom of the prongs below the small jump ring using a piercing saw (see page 22) and file to tidy.

15 Trim the prongs with a piercing saw so they are ⅛ in (3mm) long above the large jump ring and file to tidy.

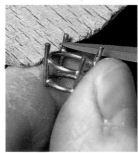

16 Use a needle file to file a "V"-shaped notch halfway down each prong, on the inner edge, for the stone to rest on.

17 Embed the setting in setter's wax on a setter's stick (see steps 15–16, page 65).

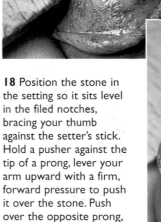

18 Position the stone in the setting so it sits level in the filed notches, bracing your thumb against the setter's stick. Hold a pusher against the tip of a prong, lever your arm upward with a firm, forward pressure to push it over the stone. Push over the opposite prong, followed by the next two. Take care to keep the table of the stone level.

19 Tidy the claw setting by filing and release it from the wax (see step 20, page 65).

Grain and pavé setting

Grain setting is a means of securing a stone without fabricating a setting. Instead, a hole is drilled or cut, the stone is placed in the hole and grains or beads of metal are raised to set the stone from the surrounding metal. This is done by cutting a piece of metal using a graver and levering it over the stone (to prepare and sharpen gravers, see pages 88–89). Grain setting is often seen where stones of the same size are set in lines.

Pearls and grain-set diamonds adorn a suite of bold gold jewelry.

YOU WILL NEED

- **Basic hand tools** (see pages 6–7)
- **Hand or pendant drill and ½₅ in (1mm) diameter twist drill bit**
- **⅛ in (3mm) flame bur**
- **Setting equipment** (see page 13)
- **Graining tool**
- **Tweezers**
- **A ring with a flat ¼ in (6mm) square center face**
- **⅛ in (3mm) diameter faceted stone**

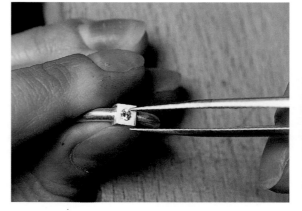

Graining tools, sometimes called beading tools, are specialist setter's tools made of steel with hemispherical indents in their ends. They are used to form the characteristic domed shape of the grains in grain setting.

1 Mark the center point on the face of the ring using dividers.

2 Drill (see pages 32–33) a ½₂ in (1mm) hole at the point marked.

3 Taper the hole using a ⅛ in (3mm) flame bur by presenting the bur to the hole vertically and opening it out. Drop the stone in the hole with tweezers—check that the table is flush with the surface of the ring face (test the level with a ruler); open the taper further if necessary.

4 Position the ring in a ring clamp and hold firmly against the bench peg, making sure the cutout braces the clamp. Hold the clamp so you keep your fingers underneath the peg.

5 Using a half-round graver, raise a grain by cutting a bead of metal. Position your thumb against the ring clamp to brace the graver. Place the graver's cutting face ⅝ in (1.5mm) from the stone at a point corresponding to the corner of the form. Hold the graver at a 45° angle and push it forward so that it digs into the metal until you are about ¼₄ in (0.5mm) from the edge of the stone. Lever your arm upward to push the resulting bead of metal over the stone.

6 Repeat step 5 on the opposite corner, then on the other two corners.

The configuration of grains can be varied either to create patterns or for greater security. Using gravers takes control and a steady hand; as grains are cut with a graver it is easy to remove the grain by mistake rather than raise it, so it may be worth practicing before you work on a final piece.

For pavé setting, grain-set stones are used to pave a surface: an opulent look is readily achieved by using a large number of relatively inexpensive small diamonds in place of a number of larger diamonds.

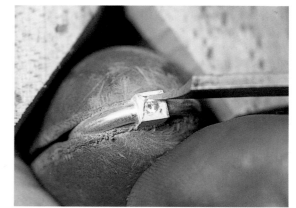

A grain set single stone on a plinth-like form is the central feature of a silver ring.

Three stones are grain set in a row to embellish the bar feature on a simple silver band.

9 Place an onglette or spitstick graver on the edge of the metal between two beads and cut the metal away, ending the cut just behind the bead. Repeat this process on the other side of the same bead. Repeat for the other three beads.

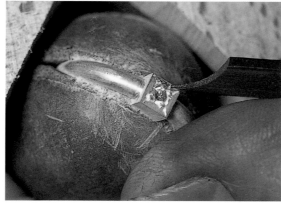

7 Using a spitstick graver in the same way as the half-round graver, cut a line from the corner of the form's surface until you reach the base of the bead, graduating the cut so the resulting groove is an elongated "V" shape.

8 Repeat on the opposite corner and then on the other two corners.

10 Using a spitstick graver, cut a chamfered face from the corners and the edge of the form to the girdle of the stone by whittling away metal from the form's edge to the stone's edge. Do not cut away any of the bead material. The process of cutting away a chamfered edge is known as thread cutting. Repeat on the other three faces.

11 Use a graining tool to form a bead into a neat dome by placing the tool on the bead and rotating it with a firm downward pressure. Repeat on the other three beads.

Carving wax for lost wax casting

Carving—usually with wax—is the process of making three-dimensional forms for casting. Modern waxes are actually plastic designed for this process. The lost wax casting process is generally a commercial service because the equipment is expensive and the process difficult to perfect. It involves attaching a sprue or feeder wire to the wax form, which is then placed in a tree formation in a

A form carved from wax is cast to make a simple signet ring.

YOU WILL NEED

- **Basic hand tools** (see pages 6–7)
- **Pendant drill and ⅛ in (3mm) diameter round bur**
- **Wax carving tools** (see page 13)
- **Wax ring blank**
- **Oval template (25° isometric)**

1 Mark out a semicircle on a wax ring blank with a pair of dividers set to ³/₃₂ in (2.5mm), using the inside edge of the wax as the guide for the dividers. Repeat on the reverse side.

2 Mark a line ⁵/₃₂ in (4mm) above the inside edge of the wax at the top of the ring using a steel ruler and a scriber. Repeat on the reverse side.

3 Join the end of the semicircle to the straight line to form the taper of the ring. Repeat on the reverse side.

4 Cut away the excess wax using a piercing saw (see pages 22–25) with a spiral saw blade for wax.

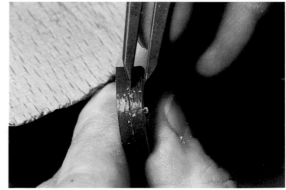

5 Define the profile by filing (see pages 28–31) with a large wax rasp, using the marked lines as a guide.

6 On the outside of the ring, mark a central line using dividers, including over the flat face. Use the flat face of the ring as a guide for the dividers.

A black diamond sits proudly supported on the shoulders of a cast white gold shank.

plastic base that is covered with an open cylinder called a flask. The tree is then embedded in plaster. The plastic base is removed before the flask is heated in a kiln, burning the wax away to leave a negative space. Molten metal is poured or thrown into the flask by a centrifugal force to fill the negative space. The flask is then plunged into cold water to release the metal forms from the plaster; the individual forms are then cut off the trunk of the tree ready for cleaning up.

Working wax is a quick process compared with working metal, so it is easier to spend time on a perfect finish in wax—clean sandpaper can be used to work and polish flat surfaces.

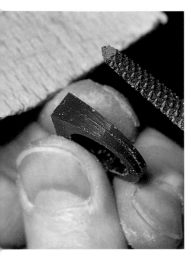

7 Taper the ring by filing the face at an angle from the base of the ring using a large wax rasp. File so you don't get too close to the guideline at the base of the ring or reduce the width at the top of the wax by breaking the top edge.

8 The top face of the ring should now be a rectangle. Mark an ellipse on the face using an oval template.

9 File the rounded form of the ring using a wax rasp, tilting the angle of the file to achieve a "D"-shaped section and remembering to file with the curve (see page 30). Take care not to break the center guideline marked earlier or you will thin the profile of the ring. File the profile at the top of the ring with care so that you define the ellipse without breaking the guideline marked in step 9.

10 Tidy up and smooth the form with hand files once the basic shape has been established. Make sure you clear the wax regularly from the file's cutting face, or it will clog.

11 Polish the surface by rubbing with fine wire wool to soften any remaining ridges left by the filing process.

12 To reduce the weight of the wax ring, hollow it out under the ellipse area using a ⅛ in (3mm) diameter bur in a pendant drill: practice on scrap wax before working on the finished ring.

13 Present the wax ring to a casting company for casting.

CARVING WAX FOR LOST WAX CARVING

Cleaning up castings

The quality of a casting can vary due to a number of factors; for example, metals behave quite differently when cast. Yellow gold generally casts well, while platinum casting is a specialist job that involves extremely high temperatures. Silver does not cast quite as well as yellow gold.

The size of the piece can also affect the outcome of the casting: smaller pieces tend to cast more successfully than large forms such as bangles. A bottleneck in the form should be avoided since this

Cast gold leaves frame stone-set buds on each of these three gold rings.

YOU WILL NEED

- **Basic hand tools (see pages 6–7)**
- **Sanding equipment (see page 82)**
- **Pendant drill with split pin and ⅛ in (3mm) round bur**
- **Ring file**
- **Cast signet ring (see pages 72–73)**

2 Trim away the remaining sprue material by cutting it off close using a piercing saw.

3 File the area where the sprue has been cut away using a hand file (see pages 28–31) to remove any traces of the sprue and restore the area to its original form. Remember to file in a sweeping action along the curve.

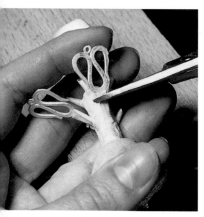

I If necessary, cut the casting from the tree form with tin snips or a piercing saw.

4 Check the shank of the casting for scratches and blemishes. File areas affected to remove deep scratches or blemishes and to define the form if necessary. Do not file the ring if the surface is blemish free: unnecessary scratches would be added by filing.

5 If the elliptical face has scratches or blemishes, file these with a hand file. Remember to place the file flat on the face so that you keep the face level and you do not create unwanted facets.

hinders flow, and you could encounter problems as a result.

Cleaning casting is far more difficult than working wax, so take time at the wax carving stage to avoid more work than is necessary once the piece is cast. The most likely problem you will have is porosity, which appears as pits in the surface of the form. These can be filed away, although they may reveal hidden porosity.

8 Clean away grit from the last sanding. Repeat step 7 using the next finest grade of paper, working in an opposing direction to the scratches left by the previous sanding.

9 Repeat step 8 until you have worked though all the grades to the finest sanding paper.

10 To clean the inside of the ring shank, repeat steps 7–9 using a sanding stick with a curved face.

6 Use the curved face of a ring file to file the inside of the ring shank to remove any scratches and blemishes. Remember to file in a sweeping action with the curve and turn the ring around so that you file through from both sides.

11 Alternatively, use a split pin with emery papers on a pendant drill to sand the inside of the ring (see pages 80–81).

7 Clean away the file marks on the shank and the elliptical face with a sanding stick, using it as you would a file. Begin with grade 150 silicone carbide paper or grade 3 emery paper. Use the stick in an opposing direction to the file marks where possible so you can see when the last set of scratches are completely removed.

12 Use a round bur on the pendant drill to clean out the hollow section of the ring. Use the bur lightly on the surface to remove any blemishes and to impart a texture. Make sure you treat the surface evenly so that you do not leave patches of the matte finish left by the casting process. Ensure you wear safety glasses to protect your eyes. The ring should now be ready for polishing.

Making a master for casting

Lost wax casting is very popular as a means of reproducing pieces because it is a relatively low-cost process where savings can be made in a number of areas. Casting grain is specifically made for casting. There is minimal work done to make grain, other than alloying, so it does not carry a heavy fashion charge, and it is cheaper than sheet and wire. Casting avoids the loss of material that tends to occur in fabrication. The same master can be used to make a casting in bronze, silver, gold, or platinum. The same master can also be modified to

YOU WILL NEED

- **Basic hand tools (see pages 6–7)**
- **Soldering equipment (see pages 10–11)**
- **Hard and medium solder**
- **Sanding equipment (see page 80)**
- **Planishing hammer**
- **Steel block**
- **⁵/₈ in (1.2mm) diameter former**
- **2 in (50mm) length of ⅛ in (3mm) diameter round wire for the sprue**
- **2¾ in (70mm) length of ³/₆₄ in (1.5mm) diameter round wire for the catch**
- **2 in (50mm) length of ¹/₃₂ in (1mm) diameter round wire for the jump ring**

I Hold a length of ³/₆₄ in (1.5mm) round wire about ¾ in (15mm) from the end with round-nosed pliers and bend the wire back on itself into a teardrop shape.

2 Holding the wire at the same level as the tip of the teardrop shape, bend it back on itself to create a second teardrop that is top to tail with the first.

3 Holding the wire at the same level as the tip of the last teardrop shape, bend it back on itself to create a third and final teardrop shape so that you create a looped "W" form.

4 Trim the ends so that they are level either side of the central loop.

5 Taper the arms of the "W" form by filing the edges with a needle file (see pages 28–31).

The same casting pattern is used to make a pendant clasp and matching pair of drop earrings.

6 Using round-nosed pliers, turn a small curl on the end of the arms so that a chain can be easily fed onto the catch.

make a number of molds with the addition of detailing like stone settings and engraving, or by the addition of fittings such as jump rings, which are more easily cut off than soldered on.

This catch is a variation on the simple "S" catch that has been used by Orientals for hundreds of years. The catch is used by pushing the arms to the side rather than pulling them apart, which would deform the shape. The "W" form keeps the catch at the front of the chain as a feature from which to hang pendants.

Casting in different materials with distinctive finishes transforms a charming pendant form.

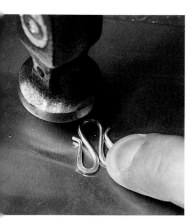

9 Close the jump ring so that it lies flat.

10 Position the jump ring at the tip of the central teardrop shape ready for soldering. Ensure that the split in the jump ring is facing toward the form so that, once soldered, the jump ring will not open.

7 To create visual interest, forge the wire (see pages 48–49) so that it widens at the curved end of each loop using a planishing hammer on a steel block. Thinning the curve on the loops of the arms will help to maintain the shape and it will also allow the arms to be moved more easily.

8 Make a small jump ring (see page 40) from 1/32 in (1mm) round wire around a 3/64 in (1.2mm) former—the smooth shank of a twist drill bit makes a good former.

11 Solder the jump ring to the form (see pages 60–61), positioning pallions of hard solder along the edge of the form where it touches the jump ring: there will be two separate areas to be soldered as solder will not run across the gap between the jump ring and the two sides of the catch.

12 Prepare a sprue (see pages 78–79) and solder, using medium or easy solder, to the master so the sprue is lying along the curve of the central hoop of the form.

13 Sand (see pages 82–83) to remove any solder or unwanted marks left as a result of forming and hammering.

14 Polish for a perfect finish to each casting (see pages 84–85).

Sprues and molds

For all forms of casting, the positioning of the sprue is important, as the sprue is the feed through which the material will flow into a form. If the sprue is too thin, the wax or metal will not flow well; bottlenecks in the form will also cause similar problems. The sprue should be positioned so that the metal flows forward into the piece. It is easier to cut off a sprue if it is sheet-like rather than round in section. Position it considering the flow but also so that it can be

YOU WILL NEED

- **Basic hand tools** (see pages 6–7)
- **Soldering equipment** (see pages 10–11)
- **Hard solder**
- **Sanding equipment** (see page 82)
- **Planishing hammer**
- **Steel block**
- **2 in (50mm) length of ⅛ in (3mm) diameter round wire**
- **Ring for spruing**

1 Anneal, pickle, and rinse (see pages 34–35) a length of wire.

2 Prepare the sprue by using a planishing hammer on the end of the ⅛ in (3mm) sprue wire onto a steel block, splaying the wire into a fan shape.

3 Mark out the profile of the base of the ring on the fanned area of the sprue.

4 Using a piercing saw (see pages 22–25), cut the sprue to match the profile of the ring base by removing the excess material beyond your guideline.

5 Match the curve of the sprue to the curve at the base of the ring by filing with hand files (see pages 28–31).

6 Solder (see pages 62–63) the sprue and ring using hard solder. If you are spruing a piece that has a lot of soldering already, consider using an easy or medium solder to avoid any of your seams and joints running or coming unsoldered. Take care to keep the join clean of surplus solder.

7 Solder again, if necessary, to fill gaps in the seam: a gap can cause an interruption in the flow between sprue and form which could make injecting wax more difficult, and casting less successful.

8 Clean up the join area by filing and sanding (see pages 82–83) if necessary, so that there is no surplus solder on the surface of the form: any blemish that appears on your master will appear on every casting.

9 Present the sprued form to a casting company to make the mold.

This unusual mold has been made by the meticulous carving of a negative ring form in a pebble.

easily removed by piercing, and so that the area where the sprue was attached can be easily filed up afterward. Spruing work for casting is best done by the maker, although casting companies do sometimes offer this service. The equipment needed for making molds is costly and cutting a mold is a specialist skill; commercial casting companies offer this service. Vulcanized rubber molds require specialist equipment; cold cure molds can be made for masters that are not metal, although this is expensive and not all casting companies offer this service.

The company will sandwich the sprued form between sheets of mold rubber in a metal mold frame. The frame and its contents are then vulcanized: heated and compressed in a press similar to an oversized flower press. The rubber is melted around the form so it fills every crevice. Once the mold has been heated sufficiently the frame is removed from the press and cooled. The rubber mold is then released from the mold frame.

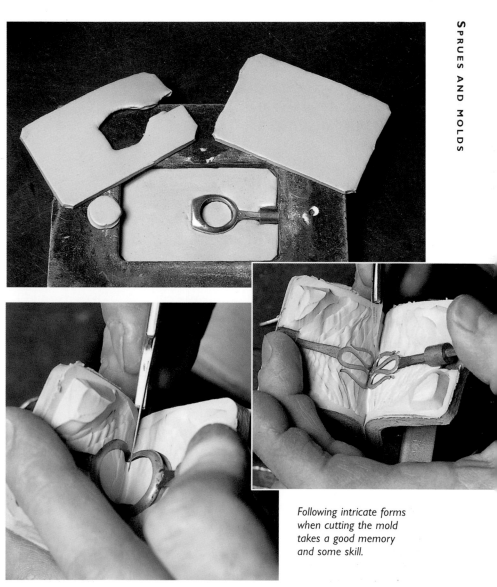

The mold is held in a bench vise and cut open using a brand new blade in a craft hinge to release the metal master inside. Notches are often cut into the top section of the mold so that the two sides of the mold locate: if the mold slips out of alignment a detectable line can appear around the form. Pressurized molten wax can now be injected into the mold to reproduce the form in wax for casting.

Following intricate forms when cutting the mold takes a good memory and some skill.

also see the following pages:
Carving wax for lost wax casting 72–73
Piercing 22–25 • **Filing** 28–31
Cleaning up castings 74–75
Sanding and cleaning up 82–83
Bezel stone setting 66–67
Annealing and pickling 34–35
Forming a ring shank 44–45
Soldering 62–63 • **Polishing** 84–85

Project 3

Stone-set ring

Wax carving is a relatively rapid and economical technique that can be used in conjunction with other techniques, such as stone setting, to create delicious, individual designs with relative ease.

YOU WILL NEED

- **Basic hand tools** (see pages 6–7)
- **Setting tools** (see page 12)
- **Soldering tools** (see page 9)
- **Hard solder**
- **Sanding equipment** (see page 80)
- **Polishing equipment** (see page 82)
- **Wax ring blank**
- **Wax carving tools** (see page 11)
- **Small mallet**
- **Ring mandrel**
- **Oval stone**
- **Paper**
- **Piece of ¹⁄₆₄ in (0.5mm) thick sheet for the bezel**
- **Piece of ³⁄₆₄ in (1.5mm) thick sheet ¹⁄₁₆ in (2mm) larger all around than the formed bezel, for the base plate**
- **Titanium sheet (optional)**

1 With dividers set to ⅛ in (3mm), mark the width of the ring on a wax ring blank. Use the inner edge of the ring as a guide for the dividers and mark both sides of the wax.

2 Cut away the material beyond the line marked using a piercing saw with a spiral saw blade for wax.

3 Tidy up the profile by filing using a large wax rasp.

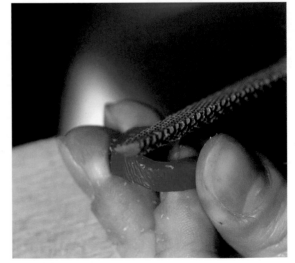

4 Using the round face of the wax rasp, file toward the center of the ring on both edges so the ring has a wavy form, as shown above.

5 File an inverted "V" form down the center of the ring all around the outside using a small wax rasp.

6 File with hand and needle files. Clean wax off the files often. Polish using fine wire wool.

7 Present the wax form to a casting company for casting.

8 Pierce off the sprue. Clean up the casting, where necessary, by filing with hand and needle files.

9 Sand the form. As shown left, clean the inside of the ring and the undulations with round-faced sanding sticks or sanding papers in a split pin with a pendant drill. Sand the "V" form with folded sanding papers.

10 Establish the height of the bezel using dividers. Place one arm at the base of the stone and set the other to a point over the curve of the stone. Measure the diameter of the stone by wrapping a strip of paper around it, and add a little extra.

11 Pierce a strip of 1/64 in (0.5mm) sheet to match the measurements taken.

12 Anneal, pickle, and rinse the strip. Prepare the join of the bezel so there is a close join for soldering, then flux and solder using hard solder.

13 Hammer the bezel circular using a small mallet and a ring mandrel.

14 Using parallel pliers, squeeze the setting into an oval to fit your stone and adjust the fit if necessary.

15 Sand the base of the bezel on a piece of coarse sanding paper supported by a sheet of glass.

16 Solder the bezel to the base plate.

17 Using a piercing saw, cut around the bezel leaving a 5/32 in (4mm) wide tab on a long edge of the stone.

18 Clean the setting by filing and sanding.

19 Curve the tab by filing so that it matches a curve on the side of the ring.

20 Solder the setting, by the curved tab, to the ring. Raise the setting for soldering, if necessary, using titanium sheet.

21 Use a setter's stick and pusher to set the stone in the bezel.

22 Warm the setter's wax over a soft flame and lever the setting out from the softened wax. Remove excess wax with acetone.

23 Finish the ring by polishing.

Sanding and cleaning up

Metal forms are cleaned up to smooth out scratches using emery papers or sticks, or silicone carbide papers. Silicone carbide is a synthetic grit that is harder wearing than the natural grit of traditional jeweler's emery papers. The grade is indicated by the number of grits in a given area; 150 is the coarsest, 1200 the finest. The latest development in sanding is a high-tech product that uses uniform grits embedded in plastic to make abrasive strips. Although expensive, this product is significantly more aggressive and longlasting.

Concentric circles make up this pendant's mesmerizing pattern, which has been sanded level at its face.

Sanding by hand

YOU WILL NEED

- **Basic hand tools (see pages 6–7)**
- **Sanding sticks made with silicone carbide papers grades 150, 220, 240, 320, 400, 600, 800, 1000, 1200, or equivalent emery papers 3, 2, 1, 0, 2/0, 3/0, 4/0**
- **Silicone carbide papers grades: 150, 220, 240, 320, 400, 600, 800, 1000, 1200 or equivalent emery papers 3, 2, 1, 0, 2/0, 3/0, 4/0**
- **Masking tape**
- **Sheet of polished glass, minimum ¼ in (5mm) thick with sanded edges**
- **Ring shank (see pages 44–45) and hollow form**

1 File (see pages 28–31) where necessary to remove scratches and blemishes or to remove excess solder.

2 Use a sanding stick in the same way as a file to begin to remove the file marks. Do not sand the entire area if it is not necessary, as you will be introducing more marks to the surface. Begin with grade 150 silicone carbide paper or grade 3 emery paper. Use the stick in an opposing direction to the file marks where possible, so that you can see when the file marks are completely removed.

3 Clean away grit from the last sanding. Repeat step 2 using the next finest grade of paper, working in an opposing direction to the scratches left by the previous sanding. Work through all the grades from coarse to fine, cleaning away grit between grades and changing the direction in which you work by 90° each time so that you can easily see when you have removed the previous set of scratches.

TIP

When cleaning up sterling/standard silver [925] that has been annealed or soldered, you will encounter firestain (an oxide that forms in the top layers of the silver as a result of heating beyond a certain temperature). After sanding and polishing, firestained silver appears as shadowed areas against the whiter silver where the firestain has been removed. Areas where the firestain has been removed show up black at the next annealing or soldering.

4 To sand flat surfaces, attach a sheet of abrasive paper to a flat surface, such as a sheet of polished glass, using masking tape around its edge. Rub the form against the abrasive paper. Work through the grades of abrasive papers as in step 3.

Sanding sticks can be made by attaching abrasive papers with double-sided tape to suitably shaped wooden dowel rods or battens. Abrasive papers can also be used by hand, giving greater flexibility to the papers and allowing access to awkward areas.

Think about cleaning up as you work. There are times when sanding needs to be planned so that it is incorporated into the jewelry-making process: when fully assembled you may not be able to reach all areas of a piece.

Sanding has been used as a way of creating texture in this imposing ring.

Pendant drill sanding

YOU WILL NEED

- **Basic hand tools (see pages 6–7)**
- **Pendant drill with split pin and abrasive rubber wheel**
- **Silicone carbide papers grades: 150, 220, 240, 320, 400, 600, 800, 1000, 1200 or equivalent emery papers 3, 2, 1, 0, 2/0, 3/0, 4/0**
- **Scissors**
- **Masking tape**
- **Ring shank (see pages 44–45) and dome**

1 To sand using a pendant drill, first file the form as usual (see step 1, **Sanding by hand**, left). Cut strips of silicone carbide paper about 1 x 6 in (25 x 150mm).

2 Load a strip into a split pin by feeding the end into the split with the abrasive surface facing you if the pin is in your right hand, shown right. If the paper is loose in the pin, fold the last ⅛in (5mm) of the strip over so that it is double the thickness, then load it

3 Wrap the paper tightly around the pin so that the abrasive surface is on the outside of the roll.

4 Wrap a strip of masking tape around the base of the roll of abrasive paper to secure it.

Grinding stones and grit-impregnated rubber can be found in a variety of shapes for cleaning up using the pendant drill.

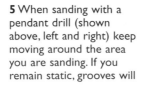

5 When sanding with a pendant drill (shown above, left and right) keep moving around the area you are sanding. If you remain static, grooves will form because of the rotary action. Work from coarse to fine paper (see step 3, **Sanding by hand**) cleaning the form between grades.

Polishing

Polishing usually describes making a smooth and glossy surface by removing material in stages of ever-decreasing scratches, until the scratches are not detectable to the naked eye. Polishing can include filing and sanding, but the term here refers to the final two stages of this process.

People often think that polishing occurs at the final stage of the making process. Although this generally happens, certain elements may need to be polished before assembly: once assembled, polishing can be

A sense of illusion is accomplished by imparting a high polish to this brooch.

Polishing by hand

YOU WILL NEED

- **Polishing threads**
- **Bristle brush**
- **Polishing sticks**
- **Tripoli**
- **Rouge**
- **Dishwashing liquid**
- **Cup hook**
- **Sanded fretwork piece (see pages 26–27 and 80–81)**

1 Wash the sanded piece with a bristle brush, dishwashing liquid, and warm water to remove traces of grit left over from sanding.

2 Rub tripoli polish onto the surface of a polishing stick.

3 Place the polishing stick flat on the surface of the piece at a 90° angle from the previous set of scratches left by sanding. Using a firm downward pressure, push the polishing stick forward on the surface of the metal.

4 Repeat this action until all the scratches left from sanding are removed, reloading the stick with tripoli frequently.

5 For some of the areas and edges that you can't reach with a polishing stick, use polishing threads. Tie a loop in the top of the threads and attach these to your bench or other suitable solid surface with a cup hook. Load the threads

with tripoli as for a stick. Pass the piece back and forth over the polishing threads to generate the polishing action. To polish in the confined spaces of fretwork, pass the threads through the holes. To polish inside a ring, use a round polishing stick.

6 Repeat step 1 to remove any traces of tripoli from the piece. The residual polish is difficult to wash away and you may find this takes longer than you expect, however, it is important that all traces are removed to avoid contaminating polishing sticks and threads used with rouge.

7 Repeat step 2 to load rouge onto a new polishing stick.

8 Place the polishing stick flat on the surface of the piece at a 90° angle from the set of scratches left by the tripoli polishing. Repeat steps 3–5 until all the tripoli scratches are removed.

9 Clean the piece as before to remove any traces of rouge. As with tripoli, the residual polish is difficult to remove and you may find this takes longer than you expect.

difficult, as polishing one element may cause unwanted wear from polishing to another adjoining part.

Polishing grits are contained in a greasy compound rather than on paper. The penultimate stage uses the coarser of the two compounds, called tripoli. The final stage uses the finest polishing compound, rouge. These two compounds can be used on most metals, although there are specialist polishing compounds available for platinum, steel, and plastic. You can buy polishing sticks or make your own by sticking felt or suede to wooden dowel rods or battens using double-sided adhesive tape.

The highly polished surface of this ring is used as a mirror to reflect the color of the feature stone.

Pendant drill polishing

YOU WILL NEED

- **Pendant drill and calico and bristle polishing bobs**
- **Bristle brush**
- **Tripoli**
- **Rouge**
- **Dishwashing liquid**
- **Sanded fretwork piece (see pages 26–27 and 80–81)**

1 Prepare the piece and load a polishing bob with tripoli following steps 1–2 of **Polishing by hand** (see left).

2 Load the bob into the pendant drill and polish by applying the bob to the surface with a firm downward pressure. Keep the bob moving over the surface to avoid wearing the surface unevenly. Take care using a pendant drill as the rotary action will cause the bob to snap on edges that are presented behind the bob if the drill is used in your right hand.

3 Repeat steps 5–9 of **Polishing by hand** using the bob and threads designed for the pendant drill.

4 Hard to reach areas can often be reached by using different attachments, such as bristle and felt bobs. There are a huge variety of shapes and sizes to choose from, such fine felt or bristle bobs for accessing tight spots, and shaped felts for polishing awkward shapes.

Silver fretwork can be used to make delicate but strong visual statements.

Metal leaf

Copper, silver, gold, and platinum are all available in a thin and paper-like leaf form to be applied as surface decoration on practically any material. Metal leaf is also used in bookbinding and restoration.

Gold metal leaf is available in different grades of fineness, and in a variety of colors from warm yellows to rose reds. Real gold is rather costly: imitation gold and silver leaf make a cheaper alternative and are especially useful for practicing with. The glue used to adhere leaf is called size and is available in a variety of drying times.

Gold leaf is used sparingly and with sensitivity to add warmth and richness to earring forms.

YOU WILL NEED
- **3 soft bristle paintbrushes**
- **Size**
- **Metal leaf, loose or transfer**
- **Face/dust mask**
- **Clear spray varnish**
- **White spirit**
- **Craft knife or scissors**
- **Tweezers, if using transfer metal leaf**
- **Twig**

2 Using the first, clean paintbrush, apply an even layer of size to the area to be gilded, shown right. Afterward, clean your paintbrush with white spirit.

3 Allow the size to dry, following manufacturer's instructions.

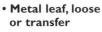

1 In a well-ventilated area away from any open flames—and wearing a dust mask—seal the surface of the twig with a clear spray sealer, applying it one layer at a time, allowing it to dry in between layers.

4 Working in a draft-free area, cut loose metal leaf with a craft knife—or transfer metal leaf with scissors—into manageable sizes.

5 If using loose leaf, brush the bristles of the second, clean paintbrush against your bare neck to create static; this will help the leaf to stick to the brush. Pick up the loose leaf on the brush and press it down onto a sized area. Apply transfer leaf using tweezers.

6 Use a clean, dry, soft bristle brush to stipple the leaf to help it adhere. Brush away excess leaf with the third paintbrush. Continue working in small areas at a time to cover the twig.

Patination: oxidizing and verdigris

Coloring the surface of metals is called patination. The effects of oxidizing and verdigris occur naturally through exposure to the elements, although they can be achieved by applying chemicals. Oxidizing causes metal to blacken, while verdigris produces a green bloom. Patination is delicate and can be affected by moisture so is unsuitable for rings. The blackening from oxidizing can be washed, but is more suitable for recessed areas. Neither oxidizing nor verdigris can withstand heat or abrasion.

Oxidizing

YOU WILL NEED
- **Soldering equipment (see pages 10–11)**
- **Protective gloves**
- **Safety goggles**
- **Paintbrush**
- **Bristle brush**
- **Soft brush**
- **Fine wire wool**
- **Wax**
- **Oxidizing solution, ⅝ in (15mm) cubed piece of potassium sulphide, ½–1 pint (275–570ml) water, and a few drops of ammonia in a Pyrex container**
- **Dishwashing liquid**
- **Formed, sanded, and polished piece of jewelry**

1 Wear protective gloves and safety goggles and work in a well-ventilated area away from foodstuffs.

2 Wash the formed piece with a bristle brush, dishwashing liquid, and warm water to completely degrease. Rinse and dry.

3 Place the piece on a clean soldering surface making sure you do not handle the metal directly.

4 Warm the piece with a soft flame from the soldering torch to accelerate the oxidizing process.

5 Remove the flame before applying the oxidizing solution with a paintbrush to the warmed metal until you achieve the color required.

6 Repeat step 2 to wash the piece.

7 Remove excess oxide with fine wire wool.

Verdigris can be added to suggest a sense of antiquity, as with this bronze brooch.

Verdigris

YOU WILL NEED
- **Soldering equipment (see pages 10–11)**
- **Protective gloves**
- **Safety goggles**
- **Paintbrush**
- **Bristle brush**
- **Soft cloth**
- **Wax**
- **Verdigris solution, 1 part cupric nitrate to 2 parts water in a Pyrex container**
- **Dishwashing liquid**
- **Formed, sanded, and polished piece of jewelry**

1 Follow steps 1–4 of **Oxidizing** (see left).

2 Remove the flame, applying the verdigris solution with a paintbrush to the warmed metal.

3 To produce a green bloom on the metal, allow the solution to dry, before adding a second application.

4 To seal the verdigris apply wax with a bristle brush and buff up with a soft cloth.

Granulation

Granulation has been used as a means of decoration for centuries, and often occurs as dense areas of grains used to create or complement an overall pattern. The grains, or beads, associated with granulation can also be used sparingly to great effect as a means of punctuating a form or surface.

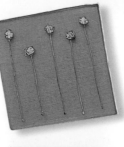

Granulation is used sparingly but decisively in a variety of ways in this series of brooches.

YOU WILL NEED

- **Basic hand tools (see pages 6–7)**
- **Charcoal block**
- **Soldering equipment (see pages 10–11)**
- **Close-meshed plastic strainer**
- **Thin scrap strip of sheet**
- **Round wire ¹⁄₃₂ in (1mm) in diameter**

2 File (see pages 28–31) a rounded end onto a thin strip of sheet and twist it into the surface of a charcoal block to make small indents to house the wire pieces. Position the holes some distance apart: if they are too close the wires may fuse together making larger grains.

3 Place a length of wire over each of the holes in the charcoal block.

5 Use a soldering torch to heat each length of wire until it melts and draws up into a ball, keeping the soldering probe on hand in case the wires move.

6 Allow the grains to cool before pickling (see steps 5–7, page 35). The size of grains makes them difficult to retrieve from pickle, so a close-meshed plastic strainer is a useful pickling aid.

Soldering granulation
Flux the grains and the surface to which the grains are to be soldered and position them on the surface. Then file solder over the grains so that there are tiny bits of solder on and between the grains. Drilling small indents into the surface helps with accurate positioning of the grains for soldering.

1 Prepare wire to be made into granules by cutting it into equal lengths. Using wire cut to a specific length will give you equal sized grains, although you can use scrap sheet if you prefer and sort the grains to size if required afterward.

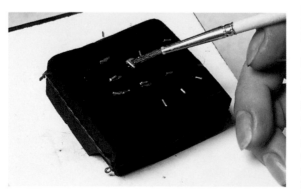

4 Flux each length of wire (see steps 1 and 4, page 60).

Reticulation

Reticulation is metal that is textured by heating until the surface has become molten. On cooling, the surface takes on a random, wrinkled pattern. Sterling silver is best suited to this process, although gold and other materials can be used. Reticulation alters the thickness of sheet because the material's surface is redistributed while molten. This can create areas of resistance noticeable during forming. The overall shape of the sheet is likely to alter so cut out your final design after reticulation to avoid your shape distorting.

Steel that has been subtly textured by reticulation is fashioned into an arresting brooch form.

YOU WILL NEED
- **Soldering equipment (see pages 10–11)**
- **Strip of silver sheet, larger than that needed for the final form**

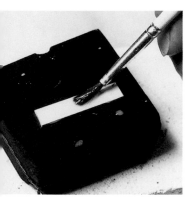

I Set up a strip of silver sheet on a soldering or charcoal block, and flux the entire surface (see steps 1 and 4, page 62). Make sure you use a creamy flux so that its chemical content is not burnt off before the surface is molten.

2 Warm the surface using a soldering torch with a hot, large flame until the flux is glassy, taking it up to temperature—when it glows bright orange —quickly so you do not burn out the flux.

3 Continue heating, taking care to watch the surface for signs of it "swimming" as it becomes molten. Soften the flame slightly so that you can control the heat and the sheet does not entirely melt.

4 Tease the molten surface by picking at it or drawing on it with a soldering probe to create peak or wave patterns.

5 When you have achieved the desired surface pattern, allow the piece to cool slightly before quenching, pickling, and rinsing (see pages 34–35).

6 Repeat steps 2–5 if you require a more textured surface.

Mill pressing

Individual textured surfaces can be achieved by compressing sheet through a rolling mill with materials such as feathers, leaves, string, and paper. These will impart their texture onto the sheet. Layering can be used to create multiple textures: a frosted background can be pressed using paper before a feather is imprinted onto the surface. Remember that, as the material and sheet are being compressed, the thickness of the sheet is likely to be decreased and the pattern elongated. Texture sheet metal before cutting it into the forms you require.

YOU WILL NEED

- **Basic hand tools (see pages 6–7)**
- **Soldering equipment (see pages 10–11)**
- **Rolling mill**
- **2 pieces of sheet, one slightly larger all around than the other**
- **Textured fabric, cutout paper motif, or feather**

1 Anneal, pickle, and rinse (see pages 34–35) the smaller piece of sheet.

2 Sandwich a textured fabric piece, paper cutout, or feather between the annealed sheet and the larger metal sheet.

3 Present the sandwich to the rollers of a rolling mill and turn the handle at the side. If the rollers offer no opposition, reduce the gap between the rollers by turning the handle on top of the mill. If you can't get the stack to feed through, increase the gap using the handle on top.

Silver can be textured and formed from simple paper cuts to create a brooch with minimal effort.

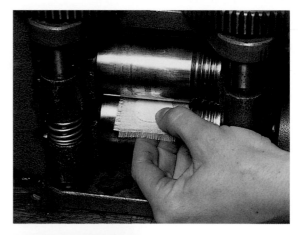

4 Check the pressure by pressing about ⅝ in (15mm) of the sandwich before reversing the action of the rollers to release it, taking care not to change the location of the stack. Carefully examine the impression. If it is right, proceed rolling at the set pressure, or adjust the rollers as before. The more pressure exerted, the more pronounced the impression.

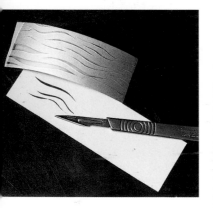

Cutting out shapes in paper with a craft knife allows you to make areas of texture and raised areas with the original sheen of the unrolled metal in the same pressing.

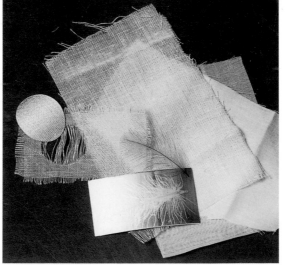

Texturing and stamping

Texturing and stamping need not be high-tech, since stamps can be made by texturing the end of a length of mild steel or by altering the working face of metal hammers. Steel hammers are not really suitable as they are made of specially hardened steel that will damage your files and other steel tools. Letter and number stamps, and steel punches used for embossing leather are available in a myriad of appealing shapes. Consider whether you are going to texture or stamp metal when planning your piece.

The modest scriber is used with precision to make a strict dot pattern on the surface of a silver pendant.

Hammered texture

YOU WILL NEED

- **Basic hand tools (see pages 6–7)**
- **Soldering equipment (see pages 10–11)**
- **Pendant drill and round bur**
- **Steel block or ring mandrel**
- **Sandbag**
- **Brass or other soft metal hammer**
- **Formed piece of jewelry**

2 A hand file can be used to cut lines into the other face of the hammer for an alternative textural effect.

3 Anneal, pickle, and rinse (see pages 34–35) the metal to be textured.

4 Support the form on the appropriate former such as a steel block, or, as here, a ring mandrel. Position the work and former on a sandbag to cushion the blow.

5 Hammer across the surface of the form with the textured hammer to impart the pattern to the metal.

Stamping

YOU WILL NEED

- **Soldering equipment (see pages 10–11)**
- **Steel block or ring mandrel**
- **Steel letter or number punch**
- **Large mallet**
- **Sandbag**
- **Marker pen (optional)**
- **Formed piece of jewelry**

Plain ring shanks can be easily decorated with words or textures to make highly individual rings.

1 Prepare the form to be stamped following steps 3–4 of **Hammered texture** (see left). If necessary, use a marker pen to mark where you want to stamp.

1 Wearing safety glasses, use a round bur with a pendant drill to grind indents into the surface of a brass or soft metal hammer face.

2 Strike a steel letter or number punch over the formed piece with a large mallet to impart the print to the metal. If you are using a number of punches to build up a word or pattern, it is a good idea to practice on scrap metal first, to accurately gauge the positioning of the characters.

Etching

Delicate etching creates a subtle textile effect on the bodies of these earrings.

The etching technique uses acid to corrode metal. The solutions used for etching metals vary: for silver, copper, gilding metal, and brass use one part nitric acid to three parts water; for steel use one part nitric acid to six parts water. Always add acid to water, not water to acid, and mix cold wearing safety goggles and protective gloves.

An etch resist is used to protect or mask areas that you do not want etched so that patterns can be formed. Etch resists can be applied to metal in various ways, including painting on as a liquid

Using an etch resist paint or pen

YOU WILL NEED

- **Etch resist paint and paintbrush or an etch resist pen**
- **Bristle brush**
- **Dishwashing liquid**
- **Piece of sheet or formed piece of jewelry**

1 Degrease the sheet or metal form using dishwashing liquid and a bristle brush in warm water. Rinse well and dry off. From now on, avoid touching any surface to be treated with resist or etched.

2 To use etch resist paint, simply paint a pattern onto the surface of the metal using a clean paintbrush. If the resist is too thick it can often be thinned, so check the manufacturer's instructions to establish the appropriate thinner. The thinner can also be used to clean the paintbrush and remove the resist after etching.

3 Leave the sheet to dry according to the manufacturer's instructions.

4 You can also draw a pattern onto the metal surface with an etch resist pen. Make sure the ink is not too thin or it may not resist the etch solution adequately.

Using etch resist film

YOU WILL NEED

- **Bristle brush**
- **Iron**
- **Craft knife**
- **Etch resist film**
- **Dishwashing liquid**
- **Piece of sheet**

1 Etch resist film can only be used on flat sheet metal. Photocopy or print your design onto the resist film according to the manufacturer's instructions.

2 Degrease the sheet following step 1 of **Using an etch resist paint or pen** (see left). Place the film emulsion-side down against the clean metal sheet on a surface suitable for ironing on.

stop-out varnish; drawing on using a fiber-tipped pen containing a resist ink; or ironed on. The latter uses a specialist resist film that needs to have high-contrast black and white images photocopied or laser printed onto it. Masking out completely with resist can, at times, be difficult. You will also find that the edges of the sheet you are working on may be partially etched, so consider etching your pattern on a sheet slightly larger than the size required, so the excess material can be cut away after etching. Remember areas covered with resist will be raised, exposed areas will be recessed.

An eye-catching organic motif etched into silver.

Etching

YOU WILL NEED

- **Safety glasses**
- **Protective gloves**
- **Nitric acid**
- **Pyrex container**
- **Plastic tongs**
- **Cloth**
- **Feather**
- **Etch resist thinner (check the manufacturer's instructions)**
- **Sheet or formed piece of jewelry treated with etch resist (see left)**

3 Start to transfer the image to the sheet by dry ironing it from the center outward, using an iron set for "cotton."

4 Now use a circular motion to iron the film from the edges toward the center. The image should appear progressively more pronounced through the film. Iron until the image appears dense black rather than blue.

5 Allow the sheet to cool completely. Use a craft knife to gently release the film and peel it away.

1 Wearing safety glasses and protective gloves, carefully and slowly add nitric acid to water in a Pyrex container to the correct ratio for the metal you are etching, as specified in the introduction above.

2 Use plastic tongs to place the metal sheet or form in the etch solution. Take care not to drop the work in as this may cause splashes. The metal will need to be immersed completely during the etching process to ensure an evenly etched surface.

3 Occasionally brush the metal surface with a feather to help distribute the etch solution.

4 Check the depth of the etched area after about five minutes. If the etched area is not deep enough, return the metal to the etch solution for a further five minutes. Repeat until the required depth is achieved.

5 Use the plastic tongs to remove the metal from the etch solution and rinse thoroughly in cold water.

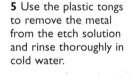

6 Remove the etch resist according to the manufacturer's instructions. This is normally done with a thinner.

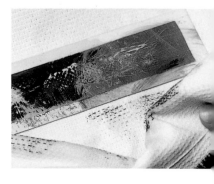

7 Use a cloth to rub away the etch resist and reveal the etched pattern.

Engraving

Engraving is the process of making marks on metal by cutting away material using sharp steel tools called gravers. To make precise patterns or formal lettering takes considerable skill and practice, however, most people, with a little time, effort, and patience, can achieve simple patterns and lettering. Try building a selection of sample sheets for practice, and devising textures and patterns that can be applied to your jewelry forms when you feel confident. The marks

This stone-set brooch is lifted out of the ordinary by the exquisite engraving.

YOU WILL NEED

- **Soldering equipment (see pages 10–11)**
- **Small mallet**
- **Polishing equipment (see page 82)**
- **Bench vise with fiber grips**
- **Sandbag**
- **³⁄₃₂ in (2.5mm) square graver**
- **Small mushroom graver handle**
- **Double-sided sharpening stone, coarse (Carborundum) and fine (India)—this must be soaked overnight in machine oil before first used**
- **Arkansas stone**
- **Piece of sheet**
- **Marker pen**
- **Masking tape**
- **Cotton wool**
- **Cloth**
- **Flat-faced block of hard wood**
- **Wintergreen or mineral oil**

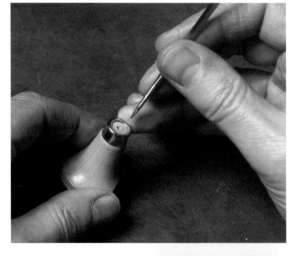

1 Using a soldering torch, heat about ⁹⁄₁₆ in (15mm) of the tang of a ³⁄₃₂ in (2.5mm) square graver to red-hot, then push it into a small mushroom graver handle.

2 Repeat step 1 until the tang is firmly in the handle. About 1 in (25mm) of the tang is burnt into the handle. Place the graver in a bench vise with fiber grips so the tang handle is upward as shown here. Allow the graver to air-cool, then tap the handle with a small mallet to secure it on the tang.

3 Cup the handle in your hand with the graver protruding from between the forefinger and thumb. Using a marker pen, make a mark on the graver about ½–³⁄₈ in (13–10mm) beyond the thumb. The length of the graver including the handle should be about 3½–4 in (90–100mm).

4 Put the graver in the vise so the point marked lies at the lip of the jaw with the tang and handle below the vise. The graver is highly tempered so it is brittle, and excess length can be broken off by a sharp tap with a small mallet. Cover the section to be broken off with a cloth to avoid flying shrapnel.

made by engraving are relatively fine and it is helpful to wear magnifying glasses while working, since this can make a significant difference.

Most shapes of graver should be sharpened to an angle of 30–45°. If the angle is more than 45° it becomes difficult to use because the tip tends to dig into the metal. If the tip becomes too long it may break off. The spitstick and oval graver should be sharpened to an angle of 60–65°.

Even an everyday form can be transformed by carefully engraved highlights.

5 Remove the graver from the vise and, using the coarse (Carborundum) face of a double-sided sharpening stone, grind its cutting face to a 45° angle. Refine it on the finer (India) face.

6 Grind away a section along the upper part of the graver using the coarse face of the sharpening stone. This reduces the area of the face to be polished and allows better visibility of the tool point during engraving. This will leave a rough stoned area, as seen in the picture above.

7 Repeat step 5 to sharpen the cutting face using an Arkansas stone, then grind away a short section of the graver under the cutting face at an angle of about 5°. Take care not to alter the shape of the point and use a drop of oil while grinding.

8 Stab the graver point into a block of hard wood to remove any burs.

9 Prepare the sheet. Metal to be engraved should normally be smooth and flat and have been treated with its final surface finish, i.e. if the piece is to be polished it should be polished before engraving (see pages 84–85).

10 Secure the metal on a block of wood using masking tape that covers about ³⁄₁₆ in (5mm) of the sheet along the entire edge.

11 Hold the graver so your thumb rests on the metal with the work supported on a sandbag, held firmly by the other hand keeping as much of the hand out of the way as possible to limit the chances of injury. Complete control of the graver takes practice; loss of control can result in injury to the hand holding the work.

12 Hold the graver at an angle, placing the point where the cut line should begin. Exert pressure and move the graver forward, away from you, to cut the metal. If the angle is too steep the graver will dig

into the metal and stop cutting, too shallow and it will tend to skip. To lengthen the line cut, use several strokes of the same depth using the graver held at the same angle. A cut should be as long as can be made in one continuous movement. For a curved cut, turn the block toward the graver as you cut forward, using your thumb as a pivot point.

13 To lubricate and prolong tool sharpness, use oil while engraving. Touch the graver tip at intervals in a wad of cotton wool saturated in wintergreen or mineral oil.

also see the following pages:
Fretwork 26–27 • **Drilling** 32–33 • **Piercing** 22–25
Filing 28–31 • **Annealing and pickling** 34–35
Doming, swaging, and drawing wire 36–37
Forging and raising 48–49 • **Soldering** 62–63
Sanding and cleaning up 82–83 • **Polishing** 84–85
Forming jump rings 82–83
Brooch pin, catch, and joint 98–99 • **Rivets** 112

Project 4

A simple suite of jewelry

A suite of jewelry can be made from the same, suitably versatile pattern. The pieces will be able to stand as individuals, although their common pattern will unite them as a suite.

YOU WILL NEED

- **Basic hand tools (see pages 6–7)**
- **Double-sided adhesive tape**
- **Scissors**
- **3 x photocopied templates**
- **Hand or pendant drill and ¹⁄₃₂ in (1mm) diameter twist drill bit**
- **Soldering equipment (see pages 10–11)**
- **Hard and medium solder**
- **Swage block**
- **Large mallet**
- **Doming block**
- **Doming punches**
- **Planishing hammer**
- **Steel block**
- **Blunt knife**
- **Sanding equipment (see page 82)**

- **Polishing equipment (see page 84)**
- **Pin vise with fiber grips**
- **Rivet equipment (see page 114)**
- **Pin hammer**
- **Sand bag**
- **³⁄₆₄ in (1.5mm) diameter former**
- **¹⁄₃₂ in (0.9mm) diameter former**
- **¹⁄₃₂ in (0.9mm) diameter ear post**
- **2¾ x 1¾ in (70 x 45mm) piece of ¹⁄₃₂ in (1mm) thick sheet**
- **Piece of 2³⁄₁₆ x ³⁄₁₆ in (55 x 5mm) ³⁄₆₄ in (1.5mm) thick sheet**
- **Titanium sheet**

(optional)
- **³⁄₃₂ in (2.5mm) sheet**
- **3½ in (90mm) length of ¹⁄₁₆ in (2mm) diameter round wire**
- **¹⁄₃₂ in (0.9mm) diameter round wire**
- **¹⁄₆₄ in (0.5mm) diameter round wire**
- **2 part epoxy adhesive**
- **2 x part-drilled stone drops**

1 Use double-sided tape to fix four photocopied templates (see below) to a 2¾ x 1¾ in (70 x 45mm) piece of ¹⁄₃₂ in (1mm) thick sheet.

2 Drill holes for piercing.

3 Using a piercing saw, cut out the internal forms of the patterns followed by the external forms.

4 File the pieces where necessary using the needle files.

5 Anneal, pickle, and rinse all four fretwork pieces.

6 Curve the largest form to make a brooch using a large gully in the swage block and the appropriate handle of a doming punch, hammering with a large mallet.

7 Curve the oval form in the same way.

Template

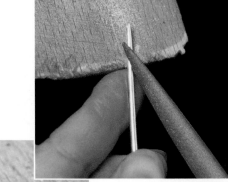

8 Curve the two small floral forms using a large indent in the doming block and the appropriate doming punch.

9 Anneal, pickle, and rinse a 3½ in (90mm) length of ¹⁄₁₆ in (2mm) diameter round wire and form it into a pin by forging it to a taper using a planishing hammer and a steel block.

10 Forge the other end to a short "V" shape, then split it by piercing a ³⁄₁₆ in (5mm) line down the center.

11 Using a blunt knife, part the split end of the pin so that the two arms fan out.

12 File the arms of the fan shape so they narrow to a point and tidy up the taper by filing.

13 Solder the oval form lengthwise to the pin using hard solder to make a hat pin.

14 Sand and polish the pin form both front and back.

15 Make two jump rings using ¹⁄₃₂ in (0.9mm) round wire over a ³⁄₆₄ in (1.5mm) diameter former. Close the jump rings.

16 File the stems of the earrings formed in step 8 so they match the curve of the jump rings.

17 Using hard solder, shown above, solder an earring to a closed jump ring so the join of the jump ring is toward the form. Repeat with the second earring.

18 Sand and polish the floral earrings both front and back.

19 Make two jump rings using ¹⁄₆₄ in (0.5mm) round wire over a ¹⁄₃₂ in (0.9mm) diameter former. Close the jump rings.

20 Solder them with a ¹⁄₃₂ in (0.9mm) diameter ear post to the center of each of the earrings.

21 Trim and file the ear posts so the ends are blunt.

22 Attach drops by twisting ¹⁄₃₂ in (0.9mm) wire to make a hoop on the end of a peg. Stick and glue the peg into a hole in the drop and leave to dry.

23 Make a brooch pin, joint, and catch for the large brooch form using ³⁄₆₄ in (1.5mm) sheet for the pin, ³⁄₃₂ in (2.5mm) sheet for the joint, and ³⁄₆₄ in (1.5mm) round wire for the catch.

24 Sand and polish the brooch form front and back.

25 Solder the joint and catch to the brooch.

26 Rivet the brooch pin in the joint using parallel pliers.

Brooch pin, catch, and joint

There are many different ways in which a brooch may be fastened, from an integral fitting on a fibula to a double pin used to fasten a piece that is particularly wide or heavy. Whatever the method used, it should be secure, while allowing the brooch to be easily taken on and off. In a simple, single brooch pin there is generally a hard piece of tapered metal or wire with a pointed end. This is attached to the brooch with a joint that allows the pin to be hinged so that it pivots open and closed. The pin is passed

A tapered silver form becomes an irresistible brooch when a brooch pin is added.

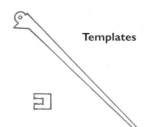

BROOCH PIN, CATCH, AND JOINT

YOU WILL NEED

- **Basic hand tools (see pages 6–7)**
- **Hand or pendant drill and ¹⁄₃₂ in (1mm) diameter twist drill bit**
- **Pin vise**
- **Soldering equipment (see pages 10–11)**
- **Hard solder**
- **Sanding and polishing equipment (see pages 82–85)**
- **Rivet equipment (see page 112)**
- **Piece of ³⁄₆₄ in (2.5 mm) thick sheet, ¼ x ¼ in (6 x 6mm)**
- **Piece of 2³⁄₈ x ³⁄₈ in (60 x 10mm) ³⁄₆₄ in (1.5mm) thick sheet**
- **1¹⁄₁₆ in (40mm) length of ³⁄₆₄ in (1.5mm) diameter round wire**
- **¹⁄₃₂ in (1mm) diameter round wire**
- **Brooch form**

Templates

1 Use a scriber and the template (below left) to mark out the brooch pin on ³⁄₆₄ in (1.5mm) sheet metal and the joint on ⁷⁄₆₄ in (2.5mm) sheet. The length of the pin is dictated by your form.

2 Pierce out the pin (see pages 22–25).

3 File away the sharp edges so that the pin is round in section (see pages 28–31).

4 Hold the pin with parallel pliers, as above, and use needle files to tidy up the wedge-shaped "stop" and the circular part of the joint section of the pin.

5 Use a scriber to mark a point in the center of the circle at the joint section of the pin for drilling.

6 Drill (see pages 32–33) the joint section of the pin at the point marked.

7 Hold the pierced joint with parallel pliers and tidy by filing with needle files.

8 Using dividers, draw a central line down the side of both arms of the joint. Use the dividers to mark a line ¹⁄₃₂ in (1mm) from the top of the joint.

9 Use the scriber to make an indent where the lines marked in step 8 cross on both arms. Drill, keeping the bit straight so the drilled holes line up when riveted.

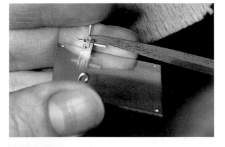

though fabric before being secured by a catch. Brooch pins generally have a slight spring action that helps keep the pin in the catch, as a sprung pin has to be depressed to be secured or released.

The open side of the catch should face the base of the brooch, allowing the pin to be secured from the underside so that the weight of the brooch helps hold the pin in the catch. In general the catch is attached on the left side of the form, with the joint on the right, although this favors right-handed people.

The double pin on this brooch form is so alluring it would be a shame to hide it.

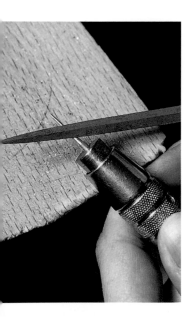

10 Make the catch by tapering a length of ³⁄₆₄ in (1.5mm) round wire using a hand file. If you have a pendant drill, hold the wire in the drill and taper it by filing while it is running. If not, hold the wire in a pin vise and file as usual.

11 Using hard solder, solder the catch wire to the back of the brooch (see pages 60–61) about ¾ of the way up the form and about ³⁄₁₆–³⁄₈ in (5–10 mm) from the edge.

12 Position the joint on the back of the brooch so the hole runs vertically, and check that the pin lies horizontal in the joint when secured in the catch. Solder the joint in place.

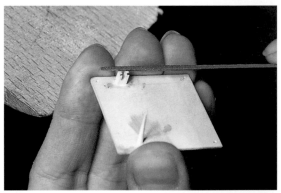

13 Round off the corners at the top of the joint arms using a needle file.

14 Turn over the catch wire using round-nosed pliers. First turn the end section into a slight curve toward the top of the form, then holding the wire ⅔ of the way down its length, turn it down toward the base of the brooch.

15 Temporarily secure the pin in the joint using a length of ¹⁄₃₂ in (1mm) round wire. Test the stop by trying to secure the pin in the catch. If it lies too high, file the wedge where it touches the joint using a needle file. Keep checking and filing the wedge until the pin can be sprung under the catch.

16 With the catch closed, check the length and trim the pin if it is too long, using top cutters, and file the tip to a point.

17 Sand and polish the pin to make it smooth (see pages 80–83).

18 Countersink the holes of the joint and rivet in the pin using ¹⁄₃₂ in (1mm) round wire (see page 114).

Box catch

A box catch has a close fitting tongue that is passed into an enclosed space. The catch is held shut because the tongue is sprung behind a specially shaped barrier plate so it is released when the tongue is depressed. If made well, a box catch is secure, longlasting, and a sophisticated solution for more costly pieces.

The success of a box catch lies in the spring action of the tongue and the fit of the tongue in the box form. If there is any movement of the tongue in the catch it will feel wobbly and weak. Closing a well-

YOU WILL NEED

- **Basic hand tools** (see pages 6–7)
- **Soldering equipment** (see pages 10–11)
- **Hard solder**
- 1⁵⁄₁₆ x ¹¹⁄₃₂ in (33 x 9mm) strip of ¹⁄₃₂ in (0.8mm) thick sheet
- ¹¹⁄₁₆ x 1³⁄₈ in (17 x 35mm) piece of ¹⁄₆₄ in (0.5mm) thick sheet
- ¹⁄₃₂ in (0.8mm) diameter former
- 4 in (10cm) length of ¹⁄₃₂ in (0.8mm) diameter round wire
- **Planishing hammer**
- **Steel block**

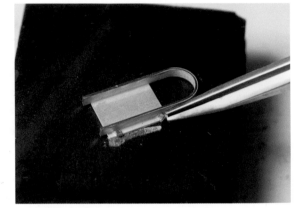

1 Set dividers to ⅛ in (3mm) and mark a 1 in (25mm) long strip on a ¹¹⁄₁₆ x 1½ in (17 x 35mm) length of ¹⁄₆₄ in (0.5mm) sheet.

2 Pierce out the strip (see pages 22–25).

3 Use needle files to file the strip (see pages 28–31) to make sure it is parallel—³⁄₃₂ in (2.5mm) wide at all points.

4 Use the dividers to mark two ⁹⁄₁₆ x ½ in (14 x 12mm) rectangles on the edges of the remaining ¹⁄₆₄ in (0.5mm) sheet. Pierce them out and file the edges square.

5 Anneal, pickle, and rinse (see pages 34–35) the strip formed in steps 1–3.

6 Using round-nosed pliers, bend the strip into a "U" shape so that both arms are parallel and measure ⅜ in (10mm) on the external edges.

7 On a soldering surface, as shown above, set up the "U"-shaped strip on top of one of the rectangles cut in step 4 so that the arms extend beyond the sheet at either end. Flux the area to be soldered and position four pallions of hard solder on the edge of the sheet, outside the area defined by the arms, one at either end of the sheet. Solder the strip to the sheet (see pages 62–63).

8 Mark a ½ x ¹⁄₃₂ in (12 x 1mm) strip on more of the ¹⁄₆₄ in (0.5mm) sheet.

9 Set the dividers to the width between the arms of the "U" form, then mark the strip to this width so it can be trimmed for soldering between the arms. Pierce out the strip, but do not cut it too short, as it is easier to file it to fit than cut another.

10 Place the newest strip between the arms of the "U" form, flush with the edge of the already soldered-on sheet. Flux the area to be soldered and position two small pallions of hard solder on the sheet at either end of the strip. Solder the strip in place.

fitted box catch should be smooth and well located with a satisfying click as the tongue springs up behind the barrier plate.

The width of the catch can be varied to suit the design of the piece of jewelry. If the box is too short or too narrow, however, the fit and the tension of the sprung tongue may be compromised.

The basic box catch can be elaborated with the addition of decorative elements such as granulation, stone settings, engraving, or piercing so that the

A simple silver box catch completes three rows of freshwater pearls to make a no-nonsense choker.

15 Use a ¹⁄₃₂ in (0.8mm) diameter former to make six jump rings from ¹⁄₃₂ in (0.8mm) round wire (see page 40). Close the jump rings so they are flat.

17 Set the dividers to ⁹⁄₁₆ in (14mm). Place one arm at the top of the sheet at the base of the jump rings and make a mark on the tongue.

11 With the dividers set to the same width as in step 9, mark a ¹⁄₃₂ in (0.8mm) strip of sheet to make the tongue of the box catch. Pierce out the tongue, making sure not to cut it too narrow since it is easier to file it to fit than cut another. File the tongue so that it will fit snugly between the arms of the "U" form. There should be no gaps between the tongue and the arms.

12 Using dividers set to ³⁄₁₆ in (5mm), mark a line across the width of the tongue at one end.

13 Using dividers set to ¹⁄₃₂ in (1mm), mark two lines on either side of the tongue from the line marked to the nearest end.

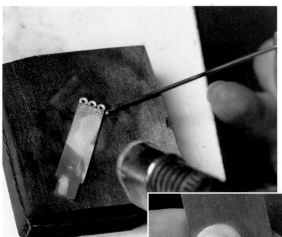

14 Pierce along the lines marked in steps 12–13 to leave a tab shape. File the tab so it is square.

16 Place three jump rings, so the joins face inward, along the wide end of the tongue on a soldering surface. Flux and position a pallion of hard solder for each jump ring. Solder the jump rings to the tongue, as shown above.

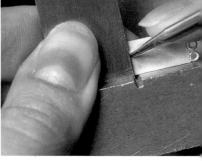

18 Using an engineer's square and a scriber, mark a line at 90° to the long edge of the tongue at the point marked in step 17.

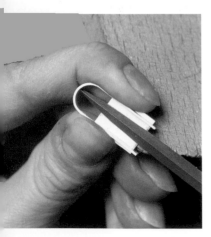

In keeping with the design of the piece, the box catch is rounded and the pusher is stone-set.

tongue can be seen through the box form. The number and style of fittings can be varied according to the requirements of the piece.

Almost any form can be used to contain a box catch, as long as the basic principles are adhered to. Think of a box catch as being similar to a piece of furniture with a secret drawer. The tongue is like a drawer that slides in and out of a piece, but the drawer or tongue can be part of a larger part of furniture. The tongue is only hinted at, rather than seen, until in use. The release

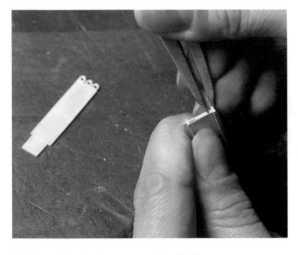

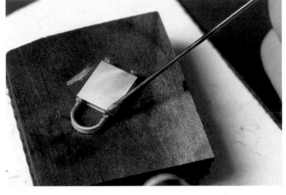

19 Using the dividers, mark the strip soldered in step 10 to make the cutout for the tab of the tongue. Set the dividers to the width of one of the filed cutouts on either side of the tab. Mark the strip using the edge of the box as a guide.

20 Use a needle file to file down the strip to the sheet, only between the lines marked in step 19. The tab of the tongue should fit snugly into the space filed—there should be no gaps between the tab and the edges of the space.

21 Position the second rectangle of sheet cut in step 4 over the "U" form so that the ends of both sheets are level. Flux the area to be soldered and position pallions of hard solder on the arms at the point where they emerge from the sheet. Solder the top sheet in place, as shown above.

22 Pierce off the protruding arms of the "U" strip.

23 File the ends of the box flush using the needle files.

24 Use dividers to mark a ³⁄₁₆ x ½ in (5 x 12mm) strip from the remaining ¹⁄₆₄ in (0.5mm) sheet. Then pierce.

25 Flux the newly cut strip, then position the open end of the box on the sheet. Position a pallion of hard solder at either end of the box on the protruding sheet. Solder the box form to the sheet.

26 File away the excess sheet surrounding the box using needle files.

27 Position the remaining three jump rings on the closed end of the box, making sure the box lies so the space for the tab is furthest from the soldering surface. Solder.

catch can be discreet to help keep the tongue hidden from view, or it can be elaborate, to hint at the presence of a catch. There are infinite possibilities, but remember, the fit must be perfect.

The box catch is masquerading as "one-of-the-beads" in this tricolor stone-set gold bracelet.

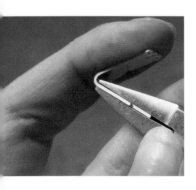

28 Use parallel pliers to bend the tongue at the line marked in step 18 to make a right angle. Take care to bend the tongue square or it will be askew when completely folded.

30 Use a planishing hammer and a steel block to flatten the tongue so that it is completely folded in half with no gaps.

31 To make the pusher, use flat-nosed pliers to bend the tab upward to a 45° angle. Lifting the tongue so the pliers can gain purchase will open the tongue so it has the spring needed to make the catch work.

32 File the pusher using a needle file so it is half its original height.

33 Pass the tongue into the box. Increase the spring if necessary by further opening the tongue.

29 Using flat-nosed pliers, bend the tongue as far as is possible.

Simple joint

Joints are a means of linking two forms, either on its own for a pendant or in succession for a bracelet or necklace. A jump ring can be used, although this is the least challenging solution. The function of the piece needs to be considered when designing a joint. A necklace needs to flex in opposing directions so that it can curve around the neck and over the shoulder, so a flexible joint may be required. The ring and ball joint demonstrated here connects lengths of wire to make up a necklace.

Quick, easy, and effective, the sliding joint supplies the movement and flexibility required for a bracelet.

YOU WILL NEED

- **Basic hand tools (see pages 6–7)**
- **Planishing hammer**
- **Steel block**
- **Soldering equipment (see pages 10–11)**
- **Hard solder**
- **¾₄ in (1.5mm) diameter former**
- **¾₄ in (1.5mm) diameter round wire**
- **½₂ in (1mm) diameter round wire**
- **Close-meshed plastic strainer**

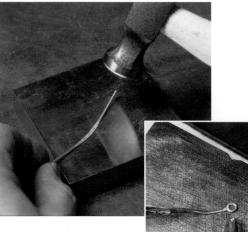

1 Using top cutters, cut 1⁹⁄₁₆ in (40mm) lengths of ¾₄ in (1.5mm) round wire.

2 Gently curve the wires by hand.

3 Using a planishing hammer and a steel block, spread the center section of each wire.

4 Use needle files to file the ends (see pages 28–31).

5 Use a ¾₄ in (1.5mm) diameter former to make jump rings from ½₂ in (1mm) round wire (see page 40). Use pliers to close the jump rings flat.

6 Using top cutters, cut ¹⁄₁₆ in (2mm) lengths of ¾₄ in (1.5mm) round wire and make these into beads following the granulation technique (see page 88).

7 Solder a jump ring to one end of a length of wire cut and flattened in steps 1–4, using hard solder (see pages 60–61). Repeat with the second length of wire and jump ring.

8 Set up the two wires so that one fits through the jump ring of the other. Flux, then position a pallion of hard solder on the end of the wire coming through the jump ring. Heat until the solder melts in place.

9 Present a fluxed bead from step 6 to the solder on the wire using sprung tweezers. Heat until the bead is soldered, removing the heat while holding the bead in position for a short while until the solder solidifies. Allow to cool, then pickle and rinse.

10 Repeat with as many wires, jump rings, and beads as necessary for your design.

Simple bail

Bails are used to hold forms such as stones so they may be hung as a pendant from a chain or as part of a larger piece. The shape and decoration of the bail can be elaborated on so that it becomes an integral element of the design, rather than just a functional addition. A simple jump ring may at times be used to replace a bail, although this is the least attractive solution. The weight and function of the piece needs to be considered when making a bail, so it is robust enough to withstand wear and tear.

A simple bail is superior to the humble jump ring, and adds the finishing touch to a beautiful piece of jade.

YOU WILL NEED

- **Basic hand tools (see pages 6–7)**
- **Pin vise**
- **Sanding equipment (see page 82)**
- **Rivet equipment (see page 112)**
- **Hand or pendant drill and ³⁄₆₄ in (1.3mm) diameter twist drill bit**
- **³⁄₆₄ in (1.2mm) outside diameter chenier**
- **1⅛ x ³⁄₁₆ in (28 x 5mm) piece of ³⁄₆₄ in (1.3mm) thick sheet**

1 Using a scriber and ruler, mark a bow tie shape on a 1⅛ x ³⁄₁₆ in (28 x 5mm) piece of sheet, ¹⁄₁₆ in (2mm) wide at the center and the full width at the ends. Join the waist of the shape to the corners with straight lines.

2 Pierce out the joint (see pages 22–25).

3 File the form to tidy it up using needle files (see pages 28–31).

4 Using dividers, mark a point ¹⁄₁₆ in (2mm) from the edge in the center of each end of the joint. Drill holes at the marked points (see pages 32–33).

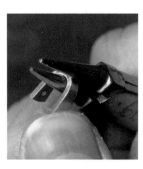

5 Using round-nosed pliers, grip the joint in the center and bend into a "U" shape.

6 Use needle files to thin the edges and create a gentle curve on the joint.

7 Remove the file marks by sanding (see pages 80–81).

8 Countersink holes for the rivet (see page 112).

9 Using dividers, measure the width of your joint at the point of the drilled holes. Add ¹⁄₃₂ in (1mm) to the dividers and mark some ³⁄₆₄ in (1.2mm) outside diameter chenier. Pierce.

10 Hold the chenier in a pin vise with ¹⁄₆₄ in (0.5mm) protruding. Flare the end by rotating a scriber in the hole of the chenier, as shown right.

11 Place the chenier through the joint and form. Flare the unflared end using a scriber with the other end supported on the bench peg to secure the rivet.

Symmetrical clasp

The function of a clasp is to join two parts, and it should be secure yet easily undone and fastened. A simple clasp can be made by positioning slits in both parts of a two-part clasp where both parts have a hole in their form: the slits are fashioned so one form can be passed over the other to link them. Many forms can be modified for this clasp, as long as the slits are positioned so they do not connect easily when worn. This can be achieved by positioning the slits at the top of the forms with the linking element to the side.

Knotted citrine beads finished with a simple symmetrical clasp.

YOU WILL NEED

- **Basic hand tools (see pages 6–7)**
- **Double-sided adhesive tape**
- **Scissors**
- **Photocopied template**
- **¹³⁄₁₆ x ⁵⁄₈ in (20 x 16mm) piece of ³⁄₆₄ in (1.2mm) thick sheet**
- **Hand or pendant drill and ³⁄₆₄ in (1.5mm) diameter twist drill bit**

1 Use double-sided tape to fix photocopies of the template to the piece of sheet (see steps 3–5, page 26).

2 Use a scriber to mark a point near the inside edge of each oval form and inside the center of the ring form on the oval end.

3 Drill holes at the points marked (see pages 32–33).

Template

4 Pierce out both oval shapes (see pages 22–25).

5 Tidy up the forms by filing with needle files (see pages 28–31). File the small ring inside and out so that the profile is rounded and will not wear threads in stringing or catch in other jump rings to which it may be attached.

6 Use a 6/0 saw blade to pierce a line through the form at the center of the long edge of the oval.

7 Hold the oval form with parallel pliers and, using a triangular needle file, begin to file one side of the slit into a "V"-shaped groove so it is no deeper than half the thickness of the sheet. Take care to keep the groove filed parallel, otherwise it will not connect well with the grooves in the other oval.

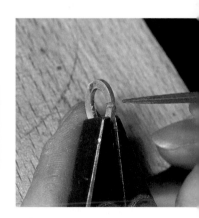

8 Flip the form and file a mirror image groove in the other side of the slit in the same way.

9 Repeat steps 7–8 on the other oval.

10 Fit the two parts together, adjusting, if necessary with further filing.

Toggle clasp

The toggle clasp involves tilting a form so it can pass through another form, then righting the first form so it is held in place. The forms used can be elaborated on so they are sophisticated by consideration to form, for example, or by the addition of stones and decorative devices.

When making a toggle clasp it is important to consider the relationship between the bar and the hole through which it will pass; if the hole is too big, or the bar too short, the toggle may come undone unexpectedly.

A toggle clasp is bold and attractive, becoming a feature as well as a functional element.

YOU WILL NEED

- **Basic hand tools (see pages 6–7)**
- **Soldering equipment (see pages 10–11)**
- **Hard solder**
- **Hand or pendant drill and ½2 in (1mm) diameter twist drill bit**
- **⅟16 in (2mm) diameter former**
- **⅛ in (3mm) diameter former**
- **³⁄64 in (5mm) diameter former**
- **¹¹⁄16 in (18mm) square of ³⁄64 in (1.2mm) thick sheet**
- **⅛ in (3mm) length of ⅛ in (3mm) inside diameter chenier**
- **1 in (24mm) length of ⅛ in (3mm) diameter round wire**
- **½2 in (1mm) diameter round wire**
- **³⁄64 in (1.5mm) diameter round wire**
- **½2 in (1.2mm) diameter round wire**
- **Length of chain (see pages 112–113)**

1 Using dividers set to ³⁄16 in (5mm), mark a circle in the center of a square of sheet. Set the dividers to ⁵⁄16 in (8mm) and mark another circle from the center.

2 Drill a hole inside the small circle (see pages 32–33).

3 Pierce out the inner circle, then the outer circle (see pages 22–25).

4 Tidy up the form by filing with a needle file (see pages 28–31).

5 File the ends of a 1 in (24mm) length of ⅛ in (3mm) round wire and the ends of a ⅛ in (3mm) length of chenier.

6 Make three jump rings (see page 40): one from ½2 in (1mm) wire on a ⅟16 in (2mm) former; one from ³⁄64 in (1.2mm) wire on a ⅛ in (3mm) former; and one from ³⁄64 in (1.5mm) wire on a ³⁄16 in (5mm) former.

7 Pass the chenier over the wire filed in step 5 so it sits in the center. Set this form up on a soldering surface with the smallest jump ring against the center of the chenier. Flux and add a pallion of hard solder to each join, then solder these forms together (see pages 62–63).

8 Attach the circle formed in steps 1–4 to a chain with the large jump ring by soldering.

9 Attach the bar to the chain with the medium jump ring by soldering.

Cuff link joints

It is essential that a cuff link joint allows for easy insertion and removal from the cuff. There are a number of different solutions to the cuff link joint, from a simple solid bar or chain link to the more complex swivel joint. Swivel cuff link joints are readily available to buy commercially, varying from a bar that turns between fixed arms to ones where the swivel and arms are attached to the link by a joint that allows the whole fitting to swivel as well. Another form of cuff link fitting is called a

A swivel joint is the perfect complement to this pair of monumental gold cuff links.

YOU WILL NEED

- **Basic hand tools (see pages 6–7)**
- **Soldering equipment (see pages 10–11)**
- **Hard solder**
- **Hand or pendant drill and $\frac{1}{32}$ in (1mm) diameter twist drill bit**
- **Rolling mill**
- **Rivet equipment (see page 112)**
- **$1\frac{3}{16}$ x $\frac{5}{8}$ in (30 x 15mm) piece of $\frac{1}{16}$ in (2mm) thick sheet**
- **$1\frac{9}{16}$ x 1 in (40 x 25mm) piece of $\frac{3}{64}$ in (1.5mm) thick sheet**
- **$\frac{1}{32}$ in (1mm) diameter round wire**

1 Using dividers, mark two $\frac{5}{8}$ in (15mm) diameter circles on $\frac{3}{64}$ in (1.5mm) thick sheet and two $\frac{1}{2}$ in (12mm) diameter circles on $\frac{1}{16}$ in (2mm) thick sheet.

2 Pierce out both sets of circles (see pages 22–25).

3 Tidy both circles by filing with a hand file (see pages 28–31).

4 Anneal, pickle, and rinse (see pages 34–35) the two circles cut from $\frac{1}{16}$ in (2mm) sheet.

5 Elongate the $\frac{1}{2}$ in (12mm) circles into $\frac{5}{8}$ in (14mm) ovals using a rolling mill (see pages 38–39).

6 On $\frac{3}{64}$ in (1.5mm) sheet, use a scriber to mark out two cuff link joints using the template below.

Template

7 Pierce out both joints and tidy by filing with hand and needle files.

8 Mark indents for drilling on the outside of both arms of the joints using a scriber, postioning the indents equidistant from the sides and the top edge.

9 Drill each arm individually (see pages 32–33). Take care to keep the drill bit straight so that the holes will line up when riveted.

10 Solder the joints to the ovals formed in step 5 using hard solder (see pages 60–61). Take care to position the joint lengthwise and centrally on the oval.

toggle fitting, as shown here, where the back pivots to allow it to be passed through the cuff.

Remember to check the orientation of the cuff link; however easy the fitting, if the back is too large for the buttonhole of the cuff, the cuff link will be difficult or impossible to use. When making a bar or chain fitting, the length between the front and back needs to be about $\frac{9}{16}$ in (18mm).

Pure in every detail, the clean lines of the toggle joint is the finishing touch for these silver cuff links.

11 Using dividers, mark a strip for the knuckles on $\frac{3}{64}$ in (1.5mm) sheet which is about $\frac{1}{16}$ in (2mm) wide and at least $\frac{5}{16}$ in (8mm) long.

12 Pierce out the strip and, holding the strip with parallel pliers, tidy by filing with a hand file.

13 Use dividers to mark two lines $\frac{5}{32}$ in (4mm) from each end of the strip.

14 Mark indents for drilling at both ends of the strip, positioning the indents equidistant from the sides and ends of the strip and drill. Take care to keep the drill bit straight.

15 Use a needle file to round off either end of the strip so it is "U" shaped in section. Take care not to file away too much as the holes should be centered in the base of the "U."

16 Pierce off the two "U" forms at the points marked in step 13.

17 Hold the forms with parallel pliers and use a needle file to file the ends just cut square.

18 Solder the knuckles to the remaining circles using hard solder. Take care to position the knuckle centrally on each circle.

19 Tidy the forms if necessary by filing with a needle file holding the form with parallel pliers.

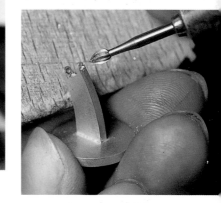

20 Countersink the holes of the joint, then rivet to the knuckle using $\frac{1}{32}$ in (1mm) round wire (see page 112).

Simple chain

The word "chain" describes a combination of linked repeated forms with flexibility and an indeterminate length. In general, the smaller the links, the more flexible the chain. Many of the chains used today are commercially made with fine wire so that they are more intricate and delicate than could be practicably made by hand.

Plain and formed jump rings are linked to make a simple chain on which to suspend a plethora of pod forms.

Basic round link chain

YOU WILL NEED

- **Basic hand tools (see pages 6–7)**
- **Rolling mill**
- **Soldering equipment (see pages 10–11)**
- **Hard solder**
- **⅛ in (3mm) diameter former**
- **¹⁄₃₂ in (1mm) diameter round wire**

1 Use ¹⁄₃₂ in (1mm) diameter round wire and a ⅛ in (3mm) diameter former to make as many jump rings as you need to form the chain (see page 40).

2 Close one jump ring flat. Flux the join, add a very small pallion of hard solder and solder without pickling afterward (see pages 62–63). Solder is easier to handle for such small joins if it is rolled thin using a rolling mill (see pages 38–39).

3 Wrap another jump ring around the first and close the join.

4 Hold the ring to be soldered with sprung tweezers so that the join is at 12 o'clock. Flux the join and add another very small pallion of thinned hard solder. Solder using a small, fine flame. Present the flame from above the jump ring and lower it until it begins to heat the top jump ring only—the ring directly below must remain unheated to prevent the two rings becoming soldered solid. Again, do not pickle a fter soldering.

5 Repeat steps 3–4 using as many jump rings as necessary for the length of chain required. Pickle and rinse to finish.

TIP
Use a solder probe to move the solder back into position if it moves as you heat.

Linked oval chain

YOU WILL NEED

- **Basic hand tools (see pages 6–7)**
- **Rolling mill**
- **Soldering equipment (see pages 10–11)**
- **Hard solder**
- **¼ in (6mm) diameter former**
- **¹⁄₁₆ in (2mm) diameter round wire**
- **³⁄₆₄ in (1.5mm) diameter round wire**

1 Use ³⁄₆₄ in (1.5mm) diameter round wire and a ¼ in (6mm) diameter former to make a number of jump rings, dependant on the length of chain you require (see page 40).

2 Use ¹⁄₁₆ in (2mm) diameter round wire and a ¼ in (6mm) diameter former to make the same amount of jump rings again. Close them flat using pliers.

A drawback of handmaking a chain is the potential tedium of the process, as each link needs to be worked, joined, and soldered individually. However, a handmade chain has its own individual character that generally outweighs the effort it takes to make. Since flexibility is of paramount importance, consider trailing a few links before you settle for an untested design, as you may otherwise face problems at a later stage.

Take two links: roll one, plain one.... the dynamics of a simple chain are born.

7 Add a second jump ring to the second oval, followed by a third oval.

3 Taking one of the closed jump rings at a time, flux the join, add a very small pallion of hard solder and solder (see pages 60–61). Solder is easier to handle for such small joins if it is rolled thin using a rolling mill (see pages 38–39). Solder all the links.

4 Roll the soldered jump rings into flat ovals using the rolling mill, until they are ¹⁵⁄₁₆ in (23mm) long.

5 Using pliers, join two ovals with a jump ring made in step 1 and close the jump ring flat.

6 Hold the jump ring to be soldered with sprung tweezers so that the join is at 12 o'clock. Flux the join and add a very small pallion of thinned solder. Solder using a small, fine flame. Present the flame from above the jump ring and lower it until it begins to heat the top ring only—the two ovals directly below must remain unheated to prevent all three elements becoming soldered solid. Use a solder probe to move the solder back into position if it moves as you heat. Do not pickle the soldering.

8 Repeat steps 6–7, adding as many links as necessary for the length of chain required and working over a soldering block as the chain gets longer. Pickle and rinse to finish.

9 Make a simple catch from one of the ovals by piercing (see pages 22–25) a slit at a right angle to the form along one of the long edges. Rolling hardens the ovals so the metal is hard enough to keep its form, yet flexible enough to be passed over a jump ring.

Rivets

Rivets are a simple means of joining two or more pieces by passing solid metal pegs or tubing through both pieces and spreading the ends to secure them. Riveting can be used to join metal to materials that can't be soldered, like wood and plastic, or for joining any materials that can't be soldered. Rivets are useful for joining enameled parts or pieces where awkward stone settings are worked and then assembled post-setting. They are also used to secure fittings where soldering would result in annealing the fitting.

A favorite photograph becomes the feature of a brooch if riveted into place.

YOU WILL NEED

- **Basic hand tools (see pages 6–7)**
- **Rivet hammer**
- **Steel block**
- **Pin vise or pendant drill and a $\frac{1}{16}$ in (2mm) flame bur**
- **Pendant drill and a $\frac{1}{32}$ in (1mm) diameter twist drill bit**
- **$\frac{1}{32}$ in (1mm) diameter round wire**
- **Forms to be joined by riveting**

3 Using top cutters, cut lengths of round wire $\frac{1}{32}$ in (1mm) longer than the sum of the parts to be joined. Cut as many lengths as there are rivets needed.

4 Put a gentle taper on the rivet wires by holding them in a pendant drill and presenting a needle file to the wire.

5 Assemble the parts to be joined and peg the drilled hole with a length of the tapered rivet wire.

7 Using a flame bur held in a pin vise or pendant drill, countersink the holes by opening their entry and exit points, rotating the bur in the hole to create a small but wide neck into which the metal rivet will be spread.

8 Insert the remaining rivet wires in the countersunk holes. Using a rivet hammer on a steel block, rivet the piece from the front by tapping a rivet head so it spreads into the countersunk area. Keep the hammer blows square to avoid damaging the material around the rivet.

1 Use a scriber to mark the points on the top piece where the rivets are to be located.

2 Assemble the parts and drill a hole on one of the points marked (see pages 32–33).

6 Drill the remaining holes at the points that are marked.

9 Turn the piece over and repeat step **8** on the rivet worked in step **8**. Repeat for each rivet.

Screws and nuts

Screws are a means of manually securing two or more pieces together. They have an advantage over rivets as the pull exerted by the screw can be adjusted and they can be removed and replaced at will. Screws and nuts are easily made using taps and dies in a variety of metals. Taps are tapered to begin cutting and nuts can take almost any form. A screw head can be almost any shape as long as it can be turned to fix the screw die flat face to the wire.

The stems of these flowers are screws that lower seeds onto the wearer's finger to change the ring size.

YOU WILL NEED

- **Basic hand tools (see pages 6–7)**
- **¹⁄₁₆ in (2mm) diameter round wire**
- **Bench vise with fiber grips**
- **¹⁄₁₆ in (2mm) die**
- **Die wrench**
- **Oil**
- **¹⁄₁₆ in (2mm) tap**
- **Tap wrench**
- **³⁄₆₄ in (1.6mm) inside diameter chenier**

1 Taper the end of a length of ¹⁄₁₆ in (2mm) round wire using a hand file.

2 Place the wire, tapered end up, in a bench vise with fiber grips.

3 Place a die in a die wrench and secure by tightening the screws. The size the screw is cut to is determined by tightening the appropriate screws on the wrench. Tightening the center screw makes a slightly larger screw; tightening the outer two screws makes a finer screw.

5 Keeping the die wrench horizontal, turn the die in a clockwise direction. For every two turns clockwise make a half turn counterclockwise. Keep turning to cut as long a length of screw as is required. When a sufficient amount is cut, turn counterclockwise until the tool is released. Release the screw from the vise.

7 Place a length of chenier vertically in the bench vise with fiber grips. The nut need not be chenier. Anything with a ³⁄₆₄ in (1.6mm) hole will do, but it must be at least ¹⁄₁₆ in (2mm) deep.

8 To cut the nut, apply oil to the tap, then present it to the chenier so the wrench is held horizontally. Proceed as in step 5, keeping the wrench level because fine taps are easily broken.

9 Repeat steps 6–8 using the bottoming/plug tap.

4 To cut the screw, apply oil to the die. Position the wrench horizontally over the wire.

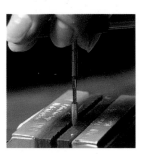

6 Load a tap into a tap wrench.

Stringing and knotting

Beads or pearls can simply be threaded tightly together, or, if the beads or pearls are particularly valuable or vulnerable, they can be separated by knots. Knotting can also be used to extend the length achieved from a limited number of beads or pearls. Pearls are also knotted to avoid damaging each other as they rub together. If pearls are to be worn daily, they should be restrung at least annually because the threads absorb oils that can result in discoloring.

The transparent citrine beads reveal the knotting with multi-colored threads.

YOU WILL NEED

- **Ruler**
- **Thread**
- **Sharp scissors or craft knife**
- **Beading needle**
- **Sewing needle**
- **Clasp (see pages 106–107)**
- **Gimp, same color as the clasp**
- **Pin vise (optional)**
- **Beads**
- **Clear nail varnish**

1 For knotting, use scissors or a craft knife to measure and cut a length of thread three times the complete length of all the beads to be used. For added interest, use several threads of different colors: the number of threads that can be used is determined by the size of the holes in the beads.

2 Pass the threads onto a beading needle. Make a loop in the other end of the thread and tie a knot to secure the loop temporarily.

3 Pass one bead onto the thread over the needle and down to the loop and knot.

4 Cut two lengths of gimp about ¼ in (6mm) long. Pass one of these over the beading needle onto the thread.

5 Pass the first part of a clasp onto the thread so it sits over the gimp, then pass the thread back through the bead.

6 Pass another bead onto the thread so the loop and knot are positioned between the two beads now strung.

7 Each time you thread on a new bead, tie a single knot after the bead, then place a sewing needle in the middle of the knot.

8 Holding the sewing needle in place, push the knot as far as possible toward the bead without overtightening it, which will make the sewing needle difficult to remove.

Various threads are available for stringing, such as pearl silk, embroidery thread, nylon, or synthetic fibers. The threads are always vulnerable to breaking. If a thread breaks where beads or pearls are strung and not knotted, there is a danger that not all the beads can be recovered. Consider using different colored threads to add color to a piece.

A mixture of stones and metal of differing shapes and sizes are strung unknotted to make a lively necklace.

9 When the knot is under the bead, pull the thread to tighten the knot around the sewing needle, maintaining an upward force toward the bead. This stops the knot from tightening at a point away from the bead as it is essential that the knot lies close to the beads. The sewing needle can be held in a pin vise for comfort.

10 Withdraw the sewing needle from the knot while continuing to tighten the knot by pulling the thread. There will be a small amount of slack released by withdrawing the needle

11 Continue passing beads onto the thread and knotting, following steps 6–10, until the knotted beads are two beads and the catch short of the length required.

12 Pass two further beads onto the thread, then add the second length of gimp.

13 Pass the second part of the clasp onto the thread. Pass the thread back through the last bead and tie a knot between the two beads.

14 Pass the thread back through the second-to-last bead.

15 Holding the threads apart, paint one side of the thread carefully with a little clear nail varnish before tying a double knot. The nail varnish will seal the knot so it will not come undone easily.

16 Trim off the excess thread. Finish off the loop tied in step 2 by carefully painting the thread nearest the base of the bead with a little clear nail varnish, then pulling on the loose end of the thread to tie a knot.

17 Separate the threads and tie again to make a double knot. Trim off the excess.

18 For stringing without knotting, measure off one and a half times the length of the beads in thread and add the beads without knots between them. Secure the last bead and clasp as you would for knotting, using gimp to protect the threads.

Knitting

Despite the fine wire used to make this tubular ring, the knitted form is strong and eminently wearable.

By knitting with metal wire, you can make physically and visually lightweight forms. The spool knitting technique makes tube forms, while knitting with straight needles (see pages 118–119) lets you make pieces of various shapes.

Knitted metal can be manipulated by pulling it into more three-dimensional forms by hand. Variations in color can be achieved by using different metals or by patinating afterward. Knitted pieces may have beads added, to create a dew-on-web effect, or pearls

Spool knitting

YOU WILL NEED

- **Basic hand tools (see pages 6–7)**
- **Wood block**
- **Hand drill**
- **⁵⁄₁₆ in (8mm) diameter twist drill bit OR a wooden cotton reel**
- **Pin hammer**
- **Tacks**
- **¹⁄₆₄ in (0.3mm) diameter round wire**
- **New soldering probe**
- **¼ in (6mm) diameter stiff rubber tubing**
- **Marker pen**
- **Ring stick**
- **Fully drilled bead**

1 You can use a wooden cotton reel, or make your own spool by drilling a ⁵⁄₁₆ in (8mm) hole in a wood block using a hand drill and twist drill bit. Use a pin hammer to hammer eight tacks equally spaced apart, all around and about ³⁄₆₄ in (1.5mm) from the edge of the hole.

2 Pass the end of a length of ¹⁄₆₄ in (0.3mm) diameter round wire down through the hole so there is about 3–4 in (75–100mm) below the block.

3 Holding the length below the block secure, begin casting on stitches, working in a clockwise direction, by passing the wire around the front of a tack and looping it around the back of the same tack, turning the loop in a counterclockwise direction.

4 Proceed to the next tack and repeat the same movement. Continue until you have cast on a complete row of stitches, then cast on one more stitch so there are two stitches on the first tack.

5 Using a new soldering probe, pick up and lift the lower of the two stitches and pass it over the first stitch, passing the stitch over the top of the tack so it is dropped into the hole.

6 Continue looping the wire around each successive tack as in step 4 and lifting the first stitch over the second stitch and tack as in step 5.

7 Repeat step 6 until the knitting is established. Pull the knitting downward as you work to pull the stitches together and stop the work from bunching.

8 When the knitting begins to protrude from below the block, pass a length of ¼ in (6mm) diameter stiff rubber tubing into the knitted form so it projects from both ends. This helps hold the shape of the tubular knitted form.

included for a touch of delicate contrast. Knitted forms can be used to contain objects, in the same way that knitted textiles can be.

Metal can be used with many knitting techniques, although it may take a little time and effort to adapt the technique so that it is easily managed. The wire needs to be very thin so that it is manageable, although it should not be too hard or too soft or it may kink excessively or be easily broken.

The three-dimensional form of this splendid pendant is cleverly knitted, no doubt with a special pattern.

9 Continue knitting with the rubber tube in place until the knitted form has reached a sufficient length to pass around the finger: in general this will be in excess of 2¾ in (70mm) so you will need to be patient. Remember to pull the knitting downward frequently as you work.

10 Bend the knitted form on the tube into a ring shape and use a marker pen to mark a point on the knitting where the end meets the rest of the knitting when it is placed at the appropriate point on a ring stick.

11 Using tin snips, cut through one strand of the wire at a point about ³⁄₁₆ in (5mm) beyond the point marked to give a length of knitting slightly longer than is required to make the ring.

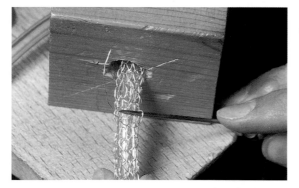

12 Use the soldering probe to unpick at least one row of stitches, then pass the loose length of knitting off the rubber tubing.

13 Join the ends of the knitting on the ring stick to check the length of knitting against the required ring size. If it is too long, unpick more stitches until it is the required length.

14 Use the loose lengths of wire at one end of the length of knitting to secure the loose stitches by threading the wire through each consecutive unsecured stitch until no open stitches remain.

15 Bring together and secure the ends of the knitting by hand, to make the ring form, threading the loose lengths of wire through the secured ends of the knitted tube. Carefully sew together the top stitches to make a continuous circle.

Knitting and simple metalwork make a charming suite of jewelry.

Knitting wire with straight needles is easy to begin with, as it is uncomplicated and versatile. With the most basic knitting technique and needles, flat forms can be easily made, while, as with knitting with yarn, the variety of patterns and forms that can be achieved is enormous.

Changing the size and the number of needles used can change the look drastically,

16 There should be two loose lengths of wire left unsecured after the form has been sewn together. Thread these to the top of the ring form if they are not already positioned there and twist them together to fasten them off.

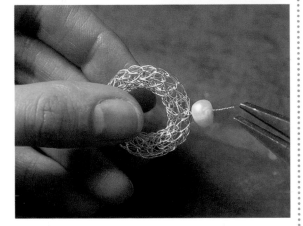

17 Pass a fully drilled bead over the twisted wires. Clip the wires ¹⁄₁₆ in (2mm) beyond the bead and use flat-nosed pliers to turn the ends over neatly and tuck them back into the hole of the bead.

Simple knitting with traditional needles

YOU WILL NEED

- **Basic hand tools (see pages 6–7)**
- **¹⁄₆₄ in (0.3mm) diameter round wire**
- **Pair of size 3 (¹⁄₈ in/3.25mm) knitting needles**

1 Hold a length of ¹⁄₆₄ in (0.3mm) diameter round wire in your left hand and create a simple loop by turning the wire over the index finger of your right hand. Place this loop onto the end of one size 3 (¹⁄₈ in/3.25mm) knitting needle.

2 Make another loop over the needle. Pick up the first loop and pass it over the second loop and the end of the needle.

3 Begin casting on stitches by using the wire in your right hand to form a loop over your index finger. Pass this loop off the finger onto the needle, then pull the thread to close the stitch

as long as the gauge of wire used is compatible with the size of needle. In order to become familiar with knitting with wire, take time to do a few test pieces with different gauges of wire and a variety of needles.

Wire can be mixed with other threads to add greater flexibility and to incorporate alternative physical and visual elements such as transparency (by using nylon) and texture (by using slub threads). A huge range of everyday materials can add color to your piece; try leather, cotton, wool, and fabric for starters.

over the needle. Do not pull the stitch too tight as a second knitting needle must be passed through the stitch in a future step. Continue casting on until you have the required number of stitches.

4 Hold the second knitting needle in your right hand and pass it through the last stitch cast on the left needle, so the right needle crosses below the left.

6 Withdraw the right needle so its tip can be passed over the left needle, catching the wire that was looped over the needle in the last step. There should now be a stitch made on the right needle.

7 Pass the right needle off the end of the left needle to drop the stitch on the left needle off its end by pushing it off with the right needle.

9 Switch the needles around so the right needle is the one with no stitches on it and repeat steps 5–8. Continue stitching and switching needles until the knitting is the required length.

11 Hold the knitting in your left hand and pass the wire through the last stitch made from the right of the stitch, then cast off the stitch.

5 Hold the wire over the forefinger of your right hand and loop it below and around the right needle. Pull the wire back to beyond the point where the needles cross.

8 Repeat steps 5–7 until you have passed off all the stitches from the left needle.

10 In preparation for casting off, using top cutters or tin snips, cut the wire so that it is double the length of the stitches on the needle.

12 Pass the wire through the cast off stitch again, and then through the next stitch on the needle to be cast off. Once secured, cast off the stitch. Continue until all the stitches are cast off and secured.

also see the following pages:
Simple knitting with traditional needles 118–119
Annealing and pickling 34–35
Forging and raising 48–49 • **Filing** 28–31
Sanding and cleaning up 82–83
Polishing 84–85 • **Bezel stone setting** 66–67
Piercing 22–25 • **Soldering** 62–63
Forming jump rings 42

Project 5

Knitted choker and stone-set clasp

Knitting is the ideal technique to use to make a choker because it is flexible and can be molded to the shape of most necks. As well, overlapping the ends allows the size to be easily altered. The addition of a stone-set spiral catch is both eye-catching and unusual.

YOU WILL NEED

- **Basic hand tools** (see pages 6–7)
- **Soldering equipment** (see pages 10–11)
- **Hard solder**
- **Raising hammer**
- **Steel block**
- **Planishing hammer**
- **Bangle mandrel**
- **Small mallet**
- **Ring mandrel**
- **Sanding equipment** (see page 80)
- **Polishing equipment** (see page 82)

- **Bench vise with fiber grips**
- **Setting tools** (see page 12)
- **¹⁄₁₆ in (2mm) diameter former**
- **Pair of size 6 (⁵⁄₃₂ in/4mm) knitting needles**
- **3⅛ x 2 x ⅜ in (80 x 50 x 10mm) block of wood**
- **³⁄₁₆ x 2 in (20 x 50mm) strip of ¹⁄₃₂ in (0.7mm) thick sheet**

- **¹³⁄₁₆ in (20mm) length of ⁵⁄₃₂ in (4mm) thick square wire**
- **⅜ in (10mm) length of ³⁄₆₄ in (1.5mm) diameter round wire**
- **¹⁄₆₄ in (0.3mm) diameter round wire**
- **⁹⁄₁₆ in (14mm) diameter cabochon stones**

1 Use ¹⁄₆₄ in (0.3mm) diameter round wire and a pair of size 6 (⁵⁄₃₂ in/ 4mm) knitting needles to knit a 16 x 4 in (40 x 10cm) strip of material.

2 Tease the form into a flared collar by extending it on the long edges by hand.

3 Anneal, pickle, and rinse a ⁵⁄₃₂ in (20mm) length of ⅛ in (4mm) thick square wire.

4 Forge the square wire to a taper using a raising hammer and a steel block.

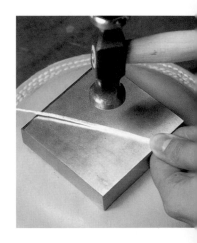

5 Anneal, pickle, and rinse again, then use a planishing hammer and a steel block to remove marks on the tapered wire made during forging.

6 Anneal, pickle, and rinse again, then shape the tapered wire into a coil by forming it around a bangle mandrel by hand.

7 Using ring-nosed pliers, hold the heavy end of the wire and pull it to the side, then into the center of the circle to create a helix form.

8 Try the catch and choker to check the shape and adjust if necessary.

9 Tidy by filing where necessary then sand and polish.

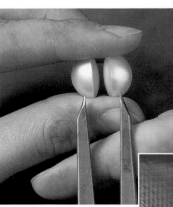

10 Hold two ⁹⁄₁₆ in (14mm) diameter cabochon stones back-to-back and establish the depth of the bezel wall using dividers.

11 Mark a ¹³⁄₁₆ x 2 in (20 x 50mm) piece of ¹⁄₃₂ in (0.7mm) thick sheet using the dividers as set in step 10. Cut off the excess by piercing.

12 Anneal, pickle, and rinse the sheet. Prepare the join of the bezel, then flux and solder using hard solder.

13 Hammer the bezel circular using a small mallet and a ring mandrel. Make adjustments to the size if necessary.

14 Pierce a disc to fit inside the setting from the remaining ¹⁄₃₂ in (0.7mm) thick sheet.

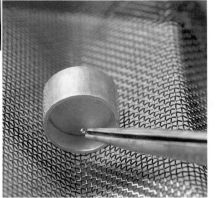

15 Position the disc in the bezel setting so it is level and central, then solder.

16 Thin the top sections of the setting wall to about ¹⁄₆₄ in (0.3mm) by filing and repeat step 9.

17 Make two jump rings from ³⁄₆₄ in (1.5mm) diameter wire and a ¹⁄₁₆ in (2mm) diameter former. Cut off and close the rings flat.

18 Position one of the jump rings on the inside of the heavy end of the wire. Seam to form and solder, then buff up with a polishing cloth.

19 Position the other jump ring centrally on the outside of the bezel setting. Join to the side and solder, then buff up using a polishing cloth.

20 Adjust the height and level the faces of the setting by filing if necessary.

21 Make a setting jig using a piercing saw to cut a close fitting hole the size of the setting in the center of a piece of wood and make a split running from the hole to the edge of the wood.

22 Put the setting in the hole so ¹⁄₃₂ in (1mm) is raised from the jig. Place in a bench vise and tighten until the setting is held firm. Set the first stone using a pusher.

23 Turn the jig over in the vise and position the second setting ¹⁄₃₂ in (1mm) raised as before, then set the other stone on the other side of the bezel. Remove from the jig and repolish where necessary.

24 Using pliers, open the jump ring, attach it to the jump ring on the spiral, and close.

Glossary

Abrasives
The natural or man-made sand-like particles used to smooth or clean away marks on a surface, as can be found adhered to abrasive papers

Acetone
A flammable liquid used to remove setters wax/cement

Adhesive
Sticky substance, such as glue, used for sticking things together

Alloy
A mixture of metals

Aluminum
A lightweight, light gray, malleable, ductile metal

Base metal
Non-precious metal such as aluminum, brass, copper, gilding metal, nickel, pewter, steel and titanium

Beveled
Slant or inclination

Bezel
The rim of metal that is used to secure a stone in rub-over setting

Bezel pusher
ALSO PUSHER
A tool used in stone setting to push metal over the stone

Blanking
Cutting

Bobs
Another term for a polishing mops used with a pendant motor or flexible shaft machine

Borax
Flux

Bronze
A pale yellow metal used for casting that is generally an alloy of copper and tin

Buffs
ALSO POLISHING MOPS
Fabric polishing end

Bullion
Gold and silver

Bur
Metal tools for grinding, for use with a pendant drill or a flexible shaft motor

Burnish
To polish by rubbing

Cabochon
An uncut, polished stone

Calipers
A tool used for the measurement of sheet, wire, and holes

Catch
A means of securing a bracelet, neckpiece or the like

Chamfer
ALSO BEVEL
Slant or inclination of a surface

Chenier
Tubing

Clasp
Another word for a catch

Claw
The name given to describe a prong used to set a stone in claw setting

Compound
ALSO POLISHING COMPOUND
Generic name for a greasy media containing abrasives used in the polishing process

Copper
A reddish-colored, malleable, ductile metal

Countersink
The enlargement of the entry to a hole

Creasing Hammer
A steel hammer with a fine cylindrical face

Cutting list
The list of materials that is made with dimensions and quantities to facilitate ordering

Die
Steel tools used for shaping by stamping or a cutting tool such as used for cutting screw threads

Die wrench
ALSO DIE STOCK
A tool for holding dies to facilitate the cutting of screws

Doming block
ALSO DAPPING BLOCK
A steel form with hemispherical depressions used to form domes

Doming punches
ALSO DAPPING PUNCHES
Steel punches with rounded heads used with a doming block to make domes

Draw
A term for pulling in, as in "drawing wire."

Drawplate
A steel tool comprising a series of tapered holes of diminishing size through which wire is pulled to transform its shape

Ductile
A term used to describe a material that is yielding or pliable

Engraving
The removal of metal using steel tools called gravers

Escapement
The name given to very small files more often used in watch making

Faceted
A term used to describe gemstones that have been cut so that their form is covered in small, polished, flat surfaces

Fashion charge
A term that refers to the additional charge on the base price of metal for transforming it into a useful format such as sheet, wire, chain, fittings, etc.

Ferrous
Containing iron

Fiber grips
Protective covering used to protect material from being damaged by the steel jaws of a vise

Fibula
A brooch where the pin is integral to the form, similar to a safety pin

Findings
A term used to describe the commercially made fittings for jewelry purposes

Finish
A term used to describe the cleaning up of a piece by sanding and polishing

Firestain
ALSO FIRESCALE
A layer of subcutaneous discoloration on sterling/standard silver that is the result of annealing or soldering

Fittings
Functional components such as catches, clips and joints as used in jewelry

Flux
The generic term used to describe a chemical used as an antioxidant as part of the soldering process

Former
A form, generally made of steel, used to support metal while it is being formed

Fretwork
A term used to describe a sheet that has been pierced with a number of holes to make an ornamental pattern

Gauge
A standard of measurement such as the thickness of sheet or the diameter of wire

Gimp
Tube made of coiled fine wire used to protect threads in stringing

Girdle
The fine line around a faceted stone where the top and bottom facets meet

Gold
The metal most commonly associated with jewelry, it is naturally found as a rich yellow color although it can be alloyed to be white, red or green in color

Grain
A term used to describe a rounded bead of metal that has been formed to hold a stone in place

Gravers
Steel tools used to cut away metal in engraving and setting

Hammer
A tool for beating or striking metal

Imperial
Non-metric standard of measure or weight

Investing
The covering of a wax form with investment powder to make a mold as part of the lost wax casting process

Investment powder
Specialist plaster used to invest wax as part of the lost wax casting process

Join
A term used to describe the meeting of two or more pieces for soldering

Joint
Another term used to describe join

Jump ring
The generic word for plain ring forms used in jewelry, not including finger rings

Karat
A measure used to express the purity of gold with 24 being the purest

Lathe
A tool used for cutting rotary objects

Malleable
A term used to describe a material that can be readily formed, rolled etc.

Mallet
Non-metal-faced hammer

Mandrel
Another name for a former

Metric
Relating to measurement based on the decimal system

Mineral oil
Oil used for lubrication in sharpening gravers

Moh's scale
A scale of approximate hardness based on resistance to abrasion

Molds
A hollow form into which molten wax or metal can be poured for casting

Nickel
A pale silvery metal also known as nickel silver

Non-ferrous
Metals not containing iron

Pallions
ALSO CHIPS
Term for pieces of solder, taken from the French word 'flake'

Patina
A surface finish that develops on metal or other material as a result of exposure to chemicals or handling

Perspex
A proprietary thermoplastic resin

Pewter
A dark gray-colored, tin-based metal that is extremely ductile

Pickle
A chemical used to remove the oxides that are a result of heating

Pin
A piece of wire with a sharpened end used to fasten an object

Planishing
Polishing or flattening by hammering with a mirror-finished hammer face

Platinum
Gray precious metal

Precious
A term used to describe diamonds, sapphires, rubies and emeralds when referring to stones or gold, silver and platinum when referring to metals

Prong
The term used to describe a tine or spur made in claw stone setting, for example

Punches
Hardened steel tools used in forming or texturing metal

Pyrex
A type of glassware resistant to heat

Rasp
A coarse file

Rivets
A bolt used to join two or more pieces

Rods
Straight solid wire

Setters cement
ALSO SETTERS WAX
A hard substance that can be softened by warming used to support jewelry pieces for stone setting

Shank
Straight or plain section of a ring or twist drill bit

Sheet
A piece of metal that is normally uniform thickness

Shot
ALSO BURNISHING MEDIA
Polished steel media used to burnish metal in barrel polishing. Solid metal shape such as pellets or spheres

Silver
A light gray metal that is malleable and ductile

Solder
A fusible alloy for joining metals

Sprue
A passage through which molten wax or metal can be poured into a mould, the wire on a casting or casting master that corresponds to the sprue passage

Sprung tweezers
ALSO CROSSLOCK TWEEZERS, SELF-LOCKING TWEEZERS OR FIBER GRIP TWEEZERS
Tweezers that close when you release them that are used as a soldering aid

Steel
A gray ferrous metal often used for tool making

Table
The top face of a faceted stone

Tallow
Rendered fat or grease

Tang
End of file, graver, tool

Taps
Tools used for cutting thread in a hole

Temper
To alter the hardness of steel

Template
A shaped, thin plate used as a guide to define a form

Thrumming
Polishing with threads

Toggle
A bar or other form used to fasten and prevent slipping through a hole

Triblet
Another term for a mandrel or former

Vernier
A sliding scale used for accurate fractional measurement

White spirit
ALSO MINERAL SPIRITS
A flammable liquid used for thinning stop out varnish for etching and for removing pitch in repoussé

Work hardening
The hardening of a material by manipulation

Wrench
ALSO STOCK
An instrument for holding taps and dies or other such equipment

Suppliers

U.S.A.

TOOLS

ALLCRAFT TOOL AND SUPPLY
666 Pacific Street
Brooklyn, NY
11207
Tel. (718) 789 2800

ANCHOR TOOL AND SUPPLY
COMPANY
PO Box 265
Chatham, NJ
Tel. (201) 887 8888

ARMSTRONG TOOL & SUPPLY
COMPANY
31747 West Eight Mile Road
Livonia, MI 48152
Tel. (800) 446 9694
Fax (248) 474 2505
Web www.armstrongtool.com

FREI & BOREL
PO Box 796
126 Second Street
Oakland, CA
94604
Tel. (510) 832 0355
Fax (800) 900 3734
Web www.ofrei.com

INDIAN JEWELER'S SUPPLY
COMPANY
601 E Coal Ave
Box 1774
Gallup, NM
87305-1774
Tel. (505) 722 4451
Fax (505) 722 4172
Web www.ijsinc.com

METALLIFEROUS
34 West 46th Street
New York, NY
10036
Tel. (212) 944 0909
Fax (212) 944 0644
Web www.metalliferous.com

MYRON TOBACK
25 West 47th Street
New York, NY
10036
Tel. (212) 398 8300
Fax (212) 869 0808
Web
www.mjsa.polygon.net/~10527

PAUL GESSWEIN AND COMPANY,
INC.
255 Hancock Ave.
PO Box 3998
Bridgeport, CT
06605-0936
Tel. (203) 366 5400
Fax (203) 366 3953

RIO GRANDE
7500 Bluewater Road NW
Albuquerque
New Mexico
Tel. 1 800 545 6566
Fax 1 800 965 2329
Web info@tbg.riogrande.com

SWEST INC.
11090 N. Stemmons Freeway
PO Box 59389
Dallas, TX
75229-1389
Tel. (214) 247 7744
Fax (214) 247 3507
Web www.swestinc.com

PRECIOUS METALS

DAVID H. FELL & COMPANY
6009 Bandini Blvd
City of Commerce, CA
90040
Tel/Fax (323) 722 6567
Web www.dhfco.com

T.B. HAGSTOZ AND SON
709 Sansom Street
Philadelphia, PA
19106
Tel. (215) 922 1627
Fax (215) 922 7126
Web
www.silversmithing.com/hagstoz

HANDY AND HARMAN
1770 Kings Highway
Fairfield, CT
06430
Tel. (203) 259 8321
Fax (203) 259 8264
Web
www.handyharmanproducts.com

HAUSER AND MILLER COMPANY
10950 Lin-Valle Drive
St. Louis, MO
63123
Tel. (800) 462 7447
Fax (800) 535 3829
Web www.hauserandmiller.com

C.R. HILL COMPANY
2734 West 11 Mile Road
Berkeley, MI
48072
Tel. (248) 543 1555
Fax (248) 543 9104
Web www.crhillcompany.com

HOOVER AND STRONG
10700 Trade Road
Richmond, VA
23236
Fax (800) 616 9997
Web
www.hooverandstrong.com

BELDEN WIRE AND CABLE
COMPANY
PO Box 1327
350 NW N Street
Richmond, IN 47374
95352-3837
Tel. (765) 962 7561
Web www.belden.com

COPPER AND BRASS

NASCO
1524 Princeton Ave.
Modesto, CA
95352-3837
Tel. (209) 529 6957
Fax (209) 529 2239

REVERE COPPER PRODUCTS
PO Box 300
Rome, NY
13442
Tel. (315) 338 2554
Fax (315) 338 2070
Web www.reverecopper.com

CANADA

TOOLS

BUSY BEE MACHINE TOOLS
2251 Gladwin Crescent
Ottawa, ON
K1B 4K9
Tel. (613) 526 4695
—OR—
1909 Oxford Street East
London, ON
N5V 2Z7
Tel. (519) 659 9868

LACY AND CO. LTD
55 Queen Street East
Toronto, ON
M5C 1R6
Tel. (416) 365 1375
Fax (416) 365 9909
Web www.lacytools.com

PRECIOUS METALS

IMPERIAL SMELTING & REFINING
CO. LTD.
451 Denison
MARKHAM, ON
L3R 1B7
Tel. (905) 475 9566
Fax (905) 475 7479
Web www.imperialproducts.com

JOHNSON MATTHEY LTD.
130 Gliddon Road
Brampton, ON
L6W 3M8
Tel. (905) 453 6120
Fax (905) 454 6869
Web www.matthey.com

UNITED KINGDOM

TOOLS

J. BLUNDELL & SONS
199 Wardour Street
London W1V 4JN
Tel. (0207) 437 4746
Fax (0207) 734 0273

BUCK & RYAN
101 Tottenham Court Road
London W1T 4DY
Tel. (0207) 636 7475
Fax (0207) 631 0726

EMC SERVICES
135 High Street
Bildeston
Ipswich
Suffolk IP7 7EL
Web emc@servs.freeserve.co

FRANK PIKE
14 Hatton Wall
Hatton Garden
London EC1N 8JH
Tel. (0207) 405 2688
Fax (0207) 831 9680

RASHBEL UK LTD
24–28 Hatton Wall
London EC1N 8JH
Tel. (0207) 831 5646
Fax (0207) 831 5647
Web www.rashbel.com
or order@rashbel.com

LE RONKA
Unit 3, Sandy Lane, Titton
Stourport-on-Severn
Worcestershire DY13 9PT
Tel. (01299) 873 600

TAYLOR DESIGNS
132 Abbotts Drive
North Wembley
Middlesex HA0 3SJ
Tel. (0208) 908 0373
Fax (0208) 8362 5013
Web Roger7@mdx.ac.uk

H.S. WALSH
234 Beckenham Road
Beckenham
Kent BR3 4TS
Tel. (0208) 778 7061
Fax (0208) 676 8669

ETCH RESIST FILM

VITRUM SIGNUM
9a North Street
Clapham Old Town
London SW4 0HN
Tel. (0207) 627 0840

PRECIOUS METALS

COOKSON PRECIOUS METALS
LTD
43 Hatton Garden
London EC1N 8EE
Tel. (0207) 400 6500
Fax (0207) 430 6511

TONY JARVIS
Suite 220, Crest Complex
Courtney Road
Gillingham
Kent ME8 0RX
Tel. (01634) 262 554
Fax (01634) 262 557
Web gold@tonyjarvis.com

JOHNSON MATTHEY METALS LTD
40-42 Hatton Garden
London EC1N 8EE
Tel. (0207) 269 8000
Fax (0207) 269 8133
Web www.matthey.com

COPPER AND BRASS

J.F. RATCLIFF (METALS) LTD.
New Summer Street
Birmingham B19 3QN
Tel. (0121) 359 5901
Fax (0121) 359 3187
Web www.jfratcliff.co.uk

J. SMITH & SONS LTD.
42-56 Tottenham Road
London N1 4BZ
Tel. (0207) 241 2430

FINDINGS

EXCHANGE FINDINGS
11-13 Hatton Wall
London EC1N 8YS
Tel. (0207) 831 7574
Fax (0207) 430 2028

H.A. LIGHT FINDINGS
Winster Grove
Kingstanding
Birmingham B44 9EQ
Tel. (0121) 360 8080
Fax (0121) 360 7730

PRIORY PRODUCTS
Findings Factory
Townfoot Estate
Brampton, Cumbria CA8 1TB
Tel. (0169) 772 944
Fax (0169) 774 1017

SAMUEL FINDINGS LTD.
14 St. Cross Street
London EC1N 8UN
Tel. (0207) 831 0657

T.H. FINDINGS
42 Hylton Street
Birmingham, West Midlands
B18 6HN
Tel. (0121) 554 9889
Fax (0121) 551 7588

GEMSTONES

CAPITAL GEMS
30B Great Sutton Street
London EC1V 0DU
Tel. (0207) 253 3575

R. HOLT & CO.
98 Hatton Garden
London EC1N 8NX
Tel. (0207) 430 5284
Fax (0207) 430 1279

LEVY GEMS
Minerva House 26-27
Hatton Garden
London EC1N 8BR
Tel. (0207) 242 4547
Fax (0207) 831 0102

—OR—
Unit 22-33 Hylton St
Hockley
Birmingham B18 6HJ
Tel. (0201) 554 4422

MANCHESTER MINERALS
Georges Rd
Stockport, Cheshire SK4 1DP
Tel. (0161) 477 0435
Fax (0161) 480 5095

PENNELLIER
28 Hatton Garden
London EC1N 8DB
Tel. (0207) 404 3100
Fax (0207) 831 7865

CASTING

CASTING HOUSE (GOLD, SILVER)
1 Augusta Street
Birmingham B18 6JA
Tel. (0121) 236 6858

WEST ONE CASTINGS
(GOLD, SILVER)
34-35 Hatton Garden
London EC1 8EB
Tel. (0207) 831 0542

WESTON BEAMOR
(PLATINUM, FINE CASTING)
3-8 Vyse Street
Birmingham B18 6LT
Tel. (0121) 236 3688
Email info@domino-wb.co.uk

AUSTRALIA

PRECIOUS METALS

A & E METAL MERCHANTS
104 Bathurst Street, 5th floor
Sydney, NSW 2000
Tel. (029) 264 5211
Fax (029) 264 7370

JOHNSON MATTHEY
(AUSTRALIA) LTD
339 Settlement Road
Thomastown, VC 3074
Tel. (039) 465 2111
Web www.matthey.com

Index

....

page numbers in *italics* refer to illustrations

Credits

Quarto would like to thank and acknowledge the following for supplying pictures and items reproduced in this book:

(Key: l left, r right, c center, t top, b bottom)

Jewelry designers

Abrams, Whitney p34t, p63t, p66t, p67tc; Appleby, Malcolm (Dr) p5tl, p26t, p94t; Barteldres, Maike p78–79t; Bolton, Amina p3tr, p35t, p118t, p119t; Chapoutot, Antoine p70t, p85t, p103t; Chen, Kuo-Jen p2tr, p3tl, p36t, p82t; Christie, Barbara p32t, p115t; Collinson, Donna p75t; De Vries Winter, Tamar p110t; Gale, Emma p2tl, p3tc, p4tr, p86t, p2tl, p3tc, p4tr, 88t; Gomez, Tamara p99t, p108t; Hinchliffe-McCutcheon, Janet p22t, p23t, p25t, p29t; Hogg, Dorothy p20t, p42t, p56t; Hopton, Martin p54t; Langton, Gilly p2b, p21tr, p28t, p35c, p62t, p91tr; Maldonado, Elizabeth p4bl, p33tc, p47t, p68t, p92t; Urino, Kyoko p3b, p21bl, p4lc, p38t, p39c, p77t, p84t, p102t, p117t; Vilhena, Manuel p3bc, p4tl, p4br, p5r, p20c, p20bl, p30t, p33tr, p44t, p52t, p83t; Watson, Zoë p53t; Wells, Paul p48t, p50t; Wood, Brian p27t.

All other jewelry designs belong to Elizabeth Olver.

Photographers

Austin, James p110t; Clark, Graham p2tl, p3tc, p4tr, p86t, p88t; Crook, Antony p2b, p28t, p35c, p62t; Degen, Joël p4bl, p32t, p33tc, p47t, p68t, p92t; Gabriner, R p66t, p67tc; Horrie p91tr; Kuniyasu p4lc, p77t, p117t; Lindsay, Philip p25t; McGregor, John K p42t, p56t; Moses, Stephen p22t, p23t, p29t; SOL p2tr, p3tl, p36t, p82t; Swann, Philippa p5tl, p26t, p94t; White, Peter p115t.

Many thanks to Rashbel UK Ltd for the photograph of the jeweler's bench (p12bl). Also, thank you to Roger Taylor of Taylor Designs for information on the RT blanking system bench and gauge (p15t).

All other photographs and illustrations are the copyright of Quarto Publishing plc.

While every effort has been made to credit contributors, Quarto would like to apologize should there have been any omissions or errors.